IMAGES
of America

RUTHERFORD COUNTY IN WORLD WAR II

VOLUME II

I0809474

More than 5,000 people from Rutherford County served with distinction during World War II. Although their roles vary, there was a shared desire. In a poem he wrote at Camp Swift, Texas, about 1943–1944, Jim Culbertson best expresses the common aim.

THE ARMY LIFE
James D. Culbertson

The army life is all the same.
We drill in the sun and sometimes rain.
We know it's hard, but it must be done
For our country's at war, and it must be won.

We're up in the morning by the bugle call.
And the sergeant shouts, "Let's get on the ball.
Let's clean these barracks. It's got to be done.
For our country's at war, and it must be won."

Then a whistle blows for reveille
Still so dark you can hardly see.
Out in the street in the ranks of fours,
And the sergeant reports, "All accounted for."

Next comes "chow." We all make a dash
To get in the line so we won't be last.
We all have hopes for something new,
But it's never different—the same old stew.

Then after chow, our work begins.
All day long, we're out and in.
It's always work and not any fun,
But we know we're at war, and it must be won.

Then after the work for the day is through,
We all sit around with nothing to do.
Just thinking of home, and our "used-to-be" fun,
But we know we're at war, and it must be won.

Now you folk back home have a job to do.
For your fighting men are depending on you.
So if you buy "bonds," we'll fire the gun
And we'll win this war that must be won.

Everyone knows what we're fighting for.
It's for peace and freedom, to stay as we are.
So let's all give a hand and get the job done,
And "Old Glory" will be waving when this war is won.

(*on the cover*) The cover photo is courtesy of Mike Davis, pictured first on the left. Sergeant Davis served with the 19th Tech, which was attached to the Third Army during its drive across France into Germany.

IMAGES
of America

RUTHERFORD COUNTY IN WORLD WAR II

VOLUME II

Anita Price Davis and James M. Walker

ARCADIA
PUBLISHING

ISBN 978-0-7385-1646-2

Published by Arcadia Publishing
Charleston, South Carolina

Printed in the United States of America

Library of Congress Catalog Card Number: 2003103772

For all general information contact Arcadia Publishing at:
Telephone 843-853-2070
Fax 843-853-0044
E-mail sales@arcadiapublishing.com
For customer service and orders:
Toll-Free 1-888-313-2665

Visit us on the Internet at www.arcadiapublishing.com

In Honor of All Rutherford County Veterans

FOREWORD

Real Heroes: Rutherford County Men Who Made the Supreme Sacrifice in World War II, by Anita Price Davis, began the story of Rutherford County in World War II by telling the stories of the 140+ men who lost their lives while in service. Local residents began to ask: "What about those who came home? May we have our stories told?" *Images of America: Rutherford County in World War II*, by Anita Price Davis and James M. Walker, preserved the accounts of Rutherford County men and women who returned from World War II and those on the home front during the 1940s. After its publication, phone calls and inquiries began to pour in from other veterans, their families, and friends who were not a part of either previous volume. Jim and Anita soon realized that one book was not enough to record the contributions of other Rutherford County residents who performed their duties responsibly and well.

The authors began to consider another volume about the roles of Rutherford County during this significant era. The county encouraged and supported our efforts. *The Daily Courier*, WCAB, WAGY, civic groups, local churches, and businesses announced interviews and data-gathering events set throughout the county. Interested individuals encouraged the attendance of veterans and their families and friends and suggested those wishing to include information bring photographs, discharge papers, and other memorabilia to tell the stories. The result of these efforts is *Rutherford County in World War II: Volume II*. To include all the veterans whom we interviewed, we had to reduce the sizes of many of the images; we regret that all citizens did not have several pages to tell their full stories.

CONTENTS

ACKNOWLEDGMENTS

The work, the support, the sharing of information and photographs, and the encouragement of others have aided in the production of *Rutherford County in World War II: Volume II*. Converse College and the administration have encouraged our endeavors. Certain individuals who have greatly facilitated the production of this work include Louise Hunt, Carolyn Wellmon, Palmer Bailey, John Dan Martin, Clarence Griffin (through his works), Billy Seay, Doug Hayes, Vanessa Harbison, Edith Owens, Jo Ann Martin, and, of course, the local churches, Jim Bishop and WCAB, Jim Brown and the *Courier*, Jean Gordon, Abbe Byers, WAGY, and, most importantly, the veterans, their families, and their friends to whom we all owe so much.

Cartha Bartlett (later Cartha Bartlett Gagan) served in the Army Nurse Corps during World War II. She remembers being one of the first to administer penicillin. First Lieutenant Bartlett served in the 165th, 203rd, and 194th General Hospitals; she served overseas in France and Belgium. She supervised three corpsmen, two civilians, and ten POWs. (Courtesy of Cartha Bartlett Gagan.)

INTRODUCTION

In the late 1930s Europe was falling under the influence of Nazism, Fascism, and Communism. The Japanese Empire, characterized by its totalitarian form of government, was striving for domination over East Asia. Ripples of this turmoil were spreading throughout the world.

America was hoping to ignore world affairs and focus on internal matters such as recovery from the Great Depression. On Sunday December 7, 1941, the Japanese attack on Pearl Harbor changed the focus of the nation.

Students who recently occupied classrooms now occupied the barracks, berths, and tents of the armed forces. Arthur Price (see next page) would soon—like many other Rutherford Countians—answer his nation's call and leave behind his wife, Nell Daves Price, and his three-month-old daughter, Anita Price, co-author of this book.

Corporal Price was one of about 5,000 Rutherford County citizens who contributed to the war effort in some capacity; this number was more than 12 percent of the total population of the county. Because North Carolina had 361,000 people who served in the military and because there were 100 counties in the state, Rutherford County sacrificially gave more than its share of enlisted men.

Corporal Price went on to make the ultimate sacrifice for his country on December 28, 1944. Four thousand eighty-eight other North Carolinians died in service also; this was more than three percent of the total Americans who died in World War II. Based on the number of counties (100) and the number from North Carolina who died in service (4,088), the number of men sacrificed from Rutherford County statistically should have been no more than 41. Instead Rutherford County lost 149 fine young men; this was more than 3.5 times its "fair" share. Indeed, the county gave sacrificially.

Throughout Rutherford County, blue stars hung in windows to denote a family member in service. Some families had more than one star on display; the McKinney family had seven sons in service. Blue stars changed to gold as telegrams and letters arrived and announced the supreme sacrifice of a loved one. Three Rutherford County families received two such notices: the Ruppe, McKinney, and Hall families sadly—but proudly—changed two blue stars in their windows to gold ones. These six real heroes were Lynn T. Ruppe (September 23, 1943) and Toy Ruppe (September 13, 1944); Daniel K. Hall (January 25, 1945) and Gilkey A. Hall Jr. (June 7, 1944); Broadus H. McKinney (December 11, 1944) and R. Earl McKinney (September 22, 1944). Tri-High School in the county sacrificed also. Seventeen young men from Tri-High School died in service of their country.

The purpose of *Rutherford County in World War II: Volume II* is to continue the stories begun in *Real Heroes: Rutherford County Men Who Made the Supreme Sacrifice during World War II* and *Rutherford County in World War II*. This book records the facts preserved through the eyes, the lives, and distinguished service of its people. We who remain must remember, and faces and facts are fast fading. This third book in the trilogy of Rutherford County in World War II will help do just that.

This Caroleen School photo from the 1930s includes Arthur Price, fourth row, fifth from the left. Price left behind his wife, Nell Daves Price, and daughter, Anita Price, co author of this book, to answer the call of World War II. (Courtesy of Jane Gurley.)

One

Pearl Harbor (1941)

Rutherford County Enters the War

On December 7, 1941, 300 Japanese naval aircraft suddenly attacked the American fleet at Pearl Harbor and the nearby Navy and Army bases. The surprise assault staggered and stunned servicemen and civilians alike. Rutherford County suffered its first fatality when the USS Arizona *sank; Mark Alexander Rhodes died as a result of the Japanese bombs.*

S/1C Mark Alexander Rhodes, of the Providence community, Forest City, Route 1, was Rutherford County's first casualty. Seaman Rhodes died in action when the USS *Arizona* sank at Pearl Harbor in the Japanese attack on December 7, 1941. (Courtesy of Jim Brown and the *Courier*.)

Recently graduated from the U.S. Naval Academy in Annapolis, Maryland, Ensign W.A. (Bill) Withrow was on board the USS *Wasp* in its homeport of Norfolk, Virginia, on December 7, 1941. The *Wasp*, a fleet carrier equipped with 84 aircraft, had returned from neutrality patrols in the North Atlantic. Following the attack on Pearl Harbor and the loss of both the USS *Lexington* at the Battle of the Coral Sea and the USS *Yorktown* at the Battle of Midway, the *Wasp* transited the Panama Canal to reach the Pacific. (Courtesy of U.S. Navy.)

Soon places like Camp Polk, Louisiana; Camp Wolters, Texas (seen on this postcard); and Fort McClellan, Alabama, became the temporary home of countless men from the county and the nation. (Courtesy of Billy Seay and Johnny Lowery.)

Two

Southwest Pacific Areas, Guadalcanal (1941)

Impeding the Japanese

As 1942 opened, the Imperial Japanese Fleet ranged with amazing swiftness over vast areas of the Western Pacific and Eastern Indian Oceans. The Japanese desire for their Greater East Asia Co-Prosperity Sphere seemed within reach. In six short months the Japanese Imperial Forces subjugated Wake Island, Hong Kong, Singapore, the Netherlands East Indies, Thailand, Burma, the Philippines, numerous other islands, and Northern New Guinea. For half a year, Emperor Hirohito's forces had run wild without impediment until the Japanese commanders became consumed with what later became known as "Victory Disease," a feeling of invincibility and inevitability. The U.S. Navy under the command of Adm. Chester Nimitz and U.S. Army in the Southwest Pacific under the command of Gen. Douglas MacArthur finally blocked further advances at Midway Island, Guadalcanal, and Southern New Guinea.

Gen. Douglas MacArthur, right, discusses the situation in the Philippines with Maj. Gen. Jonathan Wainwright. (Courtesy of U.S. Army Signal Corps.)

Pfc. James Marion Sane, 5th Marine Raiders/1st Marine Division, fought on Tulagi Island and Guadalcanal. Private Sane participated in the Battle of Edson Ridge ("Bloody Ridge") on September 14, 1942, where 850 Marines forced 3,500 Japanese troops to withdraw, saving Henderson Air Field. Private Sane received the Purple Heart for wounds received at the first Battle of Matanikau River on Guadalcanal. His division received the Presidential Unit Citation for its heroic service on Guadalcanal. (Courtesy of Robert Maurice Sane and Mrs. Marianne Sane Pfeiffer.)

Ensign Bill Withrow on board the USS *Wasp* served as Assistant Air Plot Officer. In an area known as "Torpedo Alley," the U.S. Navy lost the *Wasp* and the destroyer *O'Brien*. At the command Withrow remembers abandoning ship and the admiral stripping to his long johns before going over the side. Fortunately, destroyers were able to rescue many survivors. The *Wasp* suffered about 500 casualties. After his rescue, Ensign Withrow received repatriation to San Diego. (Courtesy of W.A. "Bill" Withrow.)

Three

THE AIR WAR IN EUROPE (1942–1945)

Bringing the War to Hitler

In July 1942 the U.S. Army Air Force started daylight bombing raids over occupied France. From bases in England, aircraft of the 8th Air Force dropped their bombs on railways, factories, and troop concentrations. The 15th Air Force from bases in North Africa and, later, Italy joined in the bombardment. The 9th Air Force, though less well known, provided tactical air support for the ground troops. These raids continued until May 1945, the end of the war in Europe.

Rutherford County natives Sgt. James Lloyd Byers, left, and his brother Sgt. Amos Bruner Byers, right, both served with the U.S. Army Air Forces. Sergeant Lloyd Byers was a flight engineer on a B-17. Sergeant Bruner Byers was a flight engineer on a C-47 engaged in glider operations; he suffered an injury during active duty and received his discharge on March 8, 1945. (Courtesy of Garland Byers and Helen Byers through Edith Owens.)

Cpl. Maurice E. Huskey, 438th Air Service Group/4th Fighter Group/8th Air Force, served at Debden Air Force Base in England. The Avondale native was a Military Policeman; he patrolled the base and helped maintain military discipline in London. (Courtesy of Maurice Huskey.)

T/Sgt. William Richard Elliott, second from right on front row, was a togglier on a B-17 and an airplane armorer. Technical Sergeant Elliott had his base at Grafton Underwood, England, where he served in the 545th Squadron/384th Bomb Group/8th Air Force. Elliott flew 35 combat missions. (Courtesy of Mark J. Elliott, son of William Richard Elliott.)

Rutherford County native Cpl. Harry G. Taylor of the 593rd AAF Base Unit/392nd Bomb Group/8th Air Force, Wendling, Norfolk, England, was an aircraft mechanic for 23 months. He and his unit serviced B-24s. One of the planes he serviced was the *Monotonous Maggie*. (Courtesy of Harry G. Taylor.)

S/Sgt. J.B. Freeman, first on the right, was the tail gunner on the *Trips Daily*, a B-24J of the 577th Squadron/392nd Bomb Group/8th Air Force, Air Station 118, Wendling, Norfolk, England. Staff Sergeant Freeman flew 31 combat missions and received credit for 1.5 kills. J.B. Freeman retired from the USAAF as a Chief Master Sergeant with the Distinguished Flying Cross, Air Medal with three oak leaf clusters, Distinguished Unit Award, and other medals. (Courtesy of D.G. "Pat" Patterson.)

Sgt. Reid H. Humphries was a supply clerk with the 85th Depot Supply Squadron. Sergeant Humphries served overseas in Bari, Italy, the site of the December 2, 1943, German raid that destroyed 42 Allied ships, killed 1,000 Allied troops and 1,000 civilians, and released a cloud of mustard gas. For his services Sergeant Humphries received the American Theater Campaign Medal, the Europe-Africa-Middle East (EAME) Campaign Medal with one Bronze Service Star, the World War II Victory Medal, and the Good Conduct Medal. (Courtesy of Reid H. Humphries.)

Sgt. James L. Harris was stationed with the 8th Army Air Force Base Depot 2, Warton Air Force Base, in England. His most vivid memory is that of a B-24 crashing into a kindergarten; the disaster killed 38 children, 3 teachers, and 30 British and American soldiers. (Courtesy of James L. Harris.)

Sgt. Wilbur Mack Withrow, an aerial gunner, flew 35 missions and earned the Distinguished Flying Cross, the Air Medal with six oak leaf clusters, and, after shot down by German fire, was a prisoner of war for several months. (Courtesy of Sarah Withrow Duncan.)

S/Sgt. Robert G. Hollifield, third from left, a waist-gunner of the 358th Squadron/303rd Bomb Group/8th Air Force, flew 31 missions over occupied Europe from May 7, 1944, to July 8, 1944, targeting industries and supporting the D-Day landings. He received the Distinguished Flying Cross, the Air Medal with three oak leaf clusters, and the EAME Campaign Medal with three Bronze Service Stars. His son writes, "My dad returned [home] a good boy transformed into a good man . . . he has never thought of his experience as something to be publicized or honored. Others were not . . . as blessed and understanding belongs only to God." (Information courtesy of Hollifield family.)

Second Lt. Thomas H. Hildebrand served with the 4th Squadron/34th Bomb Group/8th Air Force at Station 156, Mendlesham, England. Lieutenant Hildebrand flew as a bombardier on 27 combat missions over a 92-day period. He earned a promotion to First Lieutenant and returned to the United States on October 28, 1944. He completed his service at Bombardier Instructor School at Midland, Texas. (Courtesy of Thomas H. Hildebrand.)

James Hugh Searcy, 323rd Squadron/91st Bomb Group/8th Air Force, earned the rank of Staff Sergeant in the USAAF. Sergeant Searcy was a tail-gunner on a B-17 over occupied Europe. He flew seven combat missions and received the Air Medal, the EAME Campaign Medal with two Bronze Service Stars, and the Good Conduct Medal. While convalescing, he had the challenge of playing a round of golf with Ben Hogan. (Courtesy of Rebecca C. Searcy.)

Sgt. John Harvey Norville, USAAF, was an aircraft crewman. Sergeant Norville, from the Westminster community of Rutherford County, was stationed in England, like so many other county servicemen. (Courtesy of Sylvia L. Hedin.)

S/Sgt. Robert L. Moore of the 599th Squadron/397th Bomb Group/9th Air Force, flew in B-26s supporting operations in Normandy, Northern France, Ardennes, and Central Europe. The B-26s provided close tactical support to troops in the field. His assignments included air bases in Chelmsford, England; St. Quentin, France; and Venlo, Holland. Sergeant Moore earned the EAME Campaign Medal with six Bronze Service Stars and the Good Conduct Medal; his unit won the Distinguished Unit Badge. (Courtesy of Robert L. Moore.)

First Lieutenant Robert Watkins, 358th Fighter Squadron/355th Fighter Group/8th Air Force, flew a P-51 from Steeple Mordan near Cambridge, England. First Lieutenant Watkins's fighter group escorted bombers as far east as Warsaw, Poland. (Courtesy of Robert Watkins.)

Sgt. Chris Sane of the USAAF parachuted from his disabled bomber over Hamburg, Germany. Sergeant Sane was a prisoner of war for several years after his capture. His other brothers who served included James Marion Sane (Chapter 2) and Robert M. Sane (Chapter 7). (Courtesy of Robert M. Sane.)

Four

NORTHERN SOLOMON ISLANDS, NEW GUINEA (1943)

Fighting Back

After the Japanese defeat on Guadalcanal in early 1943, the United States started to clear Japanese troops from the remaining Solomon Islands. First to fall were the Russell Islands in February 1943. Next came New Georgia Island (June–July 1943), Vella Lavella Island (August 1943), and Bougainville Island (November 1943).

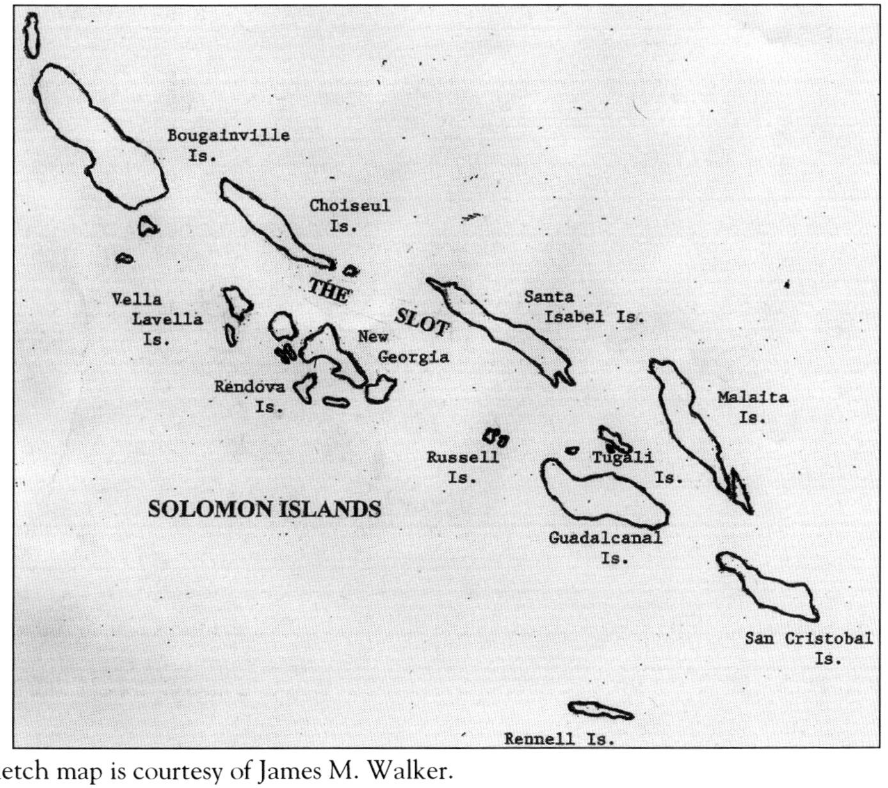

The sketch map is courtesy of James M. Walker.

Pfc. Delvo Dexter Scruggs, Headquarters Company 2nd Battalion/172nd Infantry Regiment/43rd Division, participated in the invasion of New Georgia Island. Private Scruggs recalls "hard fighting" against the Japanese. He remembers his transport receiving torpedo hits and his being in the water for 14 hours before rescue. A vivid memory of Delvo Scruggs is of being wounded in the right arm by the Japanese on Vella Lavella Island on September 5, 1943. (Courtesy of Delvo Dexter Scruggs.)

While assigned to a special platoon, Cpl. Boyd W. Luckadoo, Company D/172nd Infantry Regiment/43rd Division, assisted in the building of onshore command posts and in the construction of bombproof shelters. Luckadoo received commendations for his devotion to duty and his untiring efforts; these reflected high credit to his unit. (Courtesy of Joyce L. Luckadoo.)

Marine Pfc. Vernon Dewitt Allen took part in the invasion of Bougainville Island in November 1943. Private Allen served as a heavy machine gun crewman in the 3rd Marine Division. Private Allen also served on Guam from July through August 1944. He received his honorable discharge on October 15, 1945, at Parris Island, South Carolina. (Courtesy of Aileen H. Allen.)

T/4 Joseph D. White served as a surgical technician in the 119th Station Hospital in New Guinea. While serving, Technician White remembered a time when the hospital was overflowing with casualties; he received orders personally to take care of a soldier with appendicitis. White, without proper training, successfully performed an appendectomy and saved the man's life. A vivid memory of Tracey White's is of hearing of his father's tending to seriously burned casualties; as White moved the men, their skin peeled off in his hands. (Courtesy of Tracey White.)

Cpl. Harold H. Ruppe served as an anti-aircraft gunner. Corporal Ruppe remembers being in New Guinea and watching American soldiers marching. He asked if any of the soldiers were from North Carolina; one was from Rutherford County! It was Harold's friend Damon Huskey. Harold also remembers being in the Philippines when Gen. Douglas MacArthur returned as promised. On an April night in 1945 Harold suffered a wound in his foot from shrapnel. (Courtesy of Harold H. Ruppe.)

T/5 Damon H. Huskey served in the 389th AAA AW Battalion. For years after seeing his close friend Harold Ruppe during the New Guinea Campaign, Damon would always greet Harold with the words, "I saw you on that hill." Technician Huskey also served on the island of Morotai. Also serving with Damon Huskey were Laddie Brackett, Fred Chapman, and Rastus Smart; Huskey is second from left on the second row. (Courtesy of Marjorie Huskey.)

Pfc. Laddie Brackett, right, served in Battery C/389th AAA AW Battalion in New Guinea and Morotai Island, which the United States invaded on September 15, 1944. The men were so hungry that they shot and cooked a parrot. The unit destroyed 42 Japanese aircraft and suffered 19 KIA and 99 wounded. Laddie's daughter laughed that her father's rank upon entering service was "general farmer;" when he was discharged he was only a Private First Class. (Courtesy of Laddie Brackett.)

Pfc. Wilburn F. Harrill served in Headquarters Squadron/21st Service Group on the Bismarck Archipelago, New Guinea, and the Southern Philippines. He received the Asiatic-Pacific Campaign Medal with three Bronze Service Stars, Philippines Liberation Ribbon, and the Good Conduct Medal. His daughter noted, "he was devoted to his family, especially his mother," "he was a good baseball player," and "it was because of men like him that I was able to live in freedom." (Courtesy of Juanita H. Carver.)

Cpl. Don H. Bridges, left, Headquarters Detachment/13th Air Depot Group, served on New Caledonia and New Guinea as a clerk typist. Bridges earned the Asiatic-Pacific Campaign Medal with one Bronze Service Star, the Good Conduct Medal, and the World War II Victory Medal. His brother Hubert Bridges, right, also served in the Army. (Courtesy of Mavis Bridges.)

Cpl. John Clark Twitty, 25th Statistical Unit/USAAF, served on New Caledonia Island, Guadalcanal, the Netherlands East Indies, and the Philippines. This is a post-war photograph. (Courtesy of Mrs. John Clark Twitty.)

Cpl. James E. Hames, 120th General Hospital, still remembers with fondness the friendships and bonding within his unit. Hames recalls advancing to the front to bring back the wounded on litters; they strapped the more severely wounded to gurneys and transported them by jeep to the rear. Corporal Hames served in New Guinea and on Luzon Island. (Courtesy of James E. Hames.)

Pfc. John B. Pegram, right, Medical Department/54th General Hospital, arrived on New Guinea in April 1944. After a short stay at Milne Bay, he moved to Hollandia on the north coast. Pegram became infected with jungle rot from the tropical surroundings. He still remembers the mental and physical sufferings he endured; he speaks with praise of the care he received from the medical staff and especially from a special nurse he remembers as Miss Fannie. Private Pegram arrived home after crossing the Pacific on the USS *Comfort*. (Courtesy of John B. Pegram.)

Quartermaster 3/C Robert Oren Pace served on board an LST during operations in New Guinea. Pace had enlisted in the Navy at the age of 17. (Courtesy of Helen Byers.)

Quartermaster 3/C Robert Oren Pace had two brothers who also served during World War II. J.B. Pace, left, stationed in Maryland, served in the Navy; J.B. was born on May 12, 1921. Albert Pace, right, served in the Army; Albert was born on March 10, 1917. (Both photos courtesy of Helen Byers.)

Five

North Africa, Sicily, and Italy (1942–1945)

President Franklin Delano Roosevelt and British Prime Minister Winston Spencer Churchill believed that an invasion of North Africa should be a first step toward an invasion of Europe. This action would be the first opportunity for the young American Army to face the veteran German troops in combat. On November 8, 1942, the Allies' amphibious attacks, Operation Torch, hit three beaches: the Atlantic coast of Morocco and both Oran and Algiers in Algeria.

Pfc. Wayne Jack Grayson of the 157th Infantry Regiment/45th Division sailed from New York to Morocco in a 75-ship convoy. Private Grayson vividly remembers the extreme temperature changes in North Africa and recalls traveling by boxcar on a meter-gauge train. In Sicily, he recalls the barren landscape, the stone walls, and the iron-hard ground. Grayson heard General Patton's apology to the troops after the notorious slapping incident. His division fought in the invasion of Anzio, Italy, in an anti-tank company with a 57mm anti-tank gun. Shrapnel wounded Grayson in the right hip, leg, and knee while his unit was engaged with several German tanks in a streambed. He received treatment at the 64th General Hospital. (Courtesy of Wayne Jack Grayson.)

Rupert J. Morrow, 20th Combat Engineers, took part in Operation Torch. He participated also in the invasion of Sicily, Operation Husky. After a transfer to England, he took part in D-Day, Northern France, and the Ardennes. He received the EAME Campaign Medal with eight Bronze Service Stars. (Courtesy of Janice Morrow.)

Cpl. Jason C. Hensley, Battery C/383rd Field Artillery Battalion, was an anti-tank gun crewman who participated in operations in Tunisia, Italy, the Rhineland, and Central Europe. For his services, Corporal Hensley received the Purple Heart and the EAME Campaign Medal with five Bronze Service Stars. Also stationed in Italy was Mack Carver, one of the five Carter brothers who served from the county. (Courtesy of Bob Hensley.)

S/Sgt. Richard Woodrow Drum, 560th Army Air Forces Base Unit, was a mess sergeant. Sergeant Drum, using his culinary skills, prepared meals—both fancy and staple—for the troops. Here he has prepared a Christmas cake for the troops; the cake reads, "Peace Good Will to All." (Courtesy of Geneva Jenkins.)

Sergeant Drum was in charge of preparing a meal for President Franklin Delano Roosevelt during the presidential visit to Morocco in January 1943. The President enjoyed the meal with his entourage. (Courtesy of Geneva Jenkins.)

Pvt. Julian Astor Goode was in the Headquarters Company/1st Battalion/1st Armored Division and was a tank driver. Private Goode served in Italy and received the EAME Campaign Medal with two Bronze Service Stars. Goode entered service in 1940 and served for the duration. (Courtesy of Dorothy Goode.)

After his induction on January 13, 1943, Marion Leonard Lowe, son of Mr. and Mrs. B.H. Lowe and husband of Reba Robbins Lowe, received his commission as a second lieutenant; he completed Officer Training School at Camp Shelby, Mississippi. Lieutenant Lowe sailed from Norfolk, Virginia, to North Africa where he assumed his duties at the 114th Station Hospital. After serving in North Africa, Lowe received a transfer to Southern Italy. While there, he received a promotion to First Lieutenant. Lowe's discharge came in December 1945. (Courtesy of Reba Robbins Lowe.)

T/4 Charles D. Proctor, Company A/159th Infantry Regiment, served as a field telephone operator. He was on the beach in the invasion of Anzio. Technician Proctor served also in Naples, Rome, Southern France, the Rhineland, and Central Europe. He received the EAME Campaign Medal with five Bronze Service Stars, the Good Conduct Medal, and the World War II Victory Medal. (Courtesy of Hilda Proctor.)

S/Sgt. Francis Falsom Roberts, the leader of a light machine gun squad, earned the Silver Star Medal for his actions at Anzio. The enemy "subjected the unit to intense mortar, small arms, and artillery fire" and his gun suffered three direct hits. He remained with the weapon even though he lost all his squad members and crawled three times across open terrain to relocate the weapon despite repeated German attacks. He fired over 2,000 rounds protecting a vital approach to his company's section. Sergeant Roberts "accounted for 100 wounded and dead Germans." (Information courtesy of the *Daily Courier* and Jim Brown; photo courtesy of Francis Falsom Roberts.)

Marion Wallace Early enlisted on September 2, 1942. Early, second row, fifth from left, drove tanks in the 1st Armored Division; he had two tanks shot from under him on Anzio Beach. Wounds hospitalized him for 30 days. Others identified in the photo are R.M. Sane (front row, fifth from left), Earl Smith (front row, sixth from left), Fred Williams (front row, tenth from left), and Frank Nanney (first row, far right). (Courtesy of Marion Wallace Early.)

Pfc. William Jack Ervin, Company E/2nd Battalion/135th Infantry Regiment/34th Division, served in Southern Italy. Ervin, with a sergeant and young lieutenant, was bringing a mule train back from the Cassino front when Germans dropped mortar shells on the group, wounded Ervin in the leg, and decapitated his sergeant. Ervin received two Purple Hearts, the EAME Campaign Medal, the Good Conduct Medal, and his regiment earned the Presidential Unit Citation. Ervin remained in Italy until surrender in April 1945. (Courtesy of William Jack Ervin.)

To supply the troops at the front, units like the 557th Quartermaster Railhead Company had to move massive amounts of supplies and ordnance to the battle areas in Southern Italy. Sgt. Hyman C. Huskey, whose duty it was to expedite the delivery of these materials, received the EAME Campaign Medal, Good Conduct Medal, Purple Heart, the Distinguished Unit Badge, and the French Croix de Guerre Medal with Palm. (Courtesy of Louise W. Huskey.)

T/5 General Morgan Horton, Company B/351st Infantry Regiment, was a laundry machine operator. He served in Naples, Rome, the Northern Apennines, and the Po Valley. Technician Horton saw Mussolini's dead body displayed in Milan in late April 1945. (Courtesy of Eva Cole Horton Humphries.)

Lloyd Vance Silver, left, served with the Army in Italy. Silver was in the infantry; he received the EAME Campaign Medal with three Bronze Service Stars and the Good Conduct Medal. He became a minister after the war. Pictured with Silver is First Sergeant Hobert L. Daniel (right), 30th Division, who also served in the Army; his stations were North Africa, Italy, Corsica, and Southern France. Daniel earned the American Campaign Medal, the EAME Campaign Medal with two Bronze Service Stars, the World War II Victory Medal, and the Good Conduct Medal. (Information courtesy of his wife Mary Daniel; photo of Silver courtesy of Gertrude Silver.)

T/Sgt. Joe Bert Moore, 3255th Company/605th Ordnance Base Armament Maintenance Battalion, served in Italy as a stock control section chief. Sergeant Moore received the EAME Campaign Medal with one Bronze Service Star. Sergeant Moore served from 1942 through 1944. (Courtesy of Evelyn W. Moore.)

Pfc. Doyle B. Jones, Company C/133rd Infantry Regiment/34th Division, was a supply clerk. Private Jones served in Sicily and Italy. He earned the American Theater Service Medal, the EAME Campaign Medal with one Bronze Service Star, the Good Conduct Medal, and the World War II Victory Medal. His brother Howard was killed in Italy; the book *Real Heroes*, by Anita Price Davis, contains details of this highly decorated soldier. (Courtesy of Mrs. Virginia Jones.)

Pfc. Joshua J. Allen, SV Company/60th Infantry Regiment, was a truck driver and served in Rome, the Arno Campaign, Southern France, the Rhineland, and Central Europe. He received the Combat Infantryman's Badge, the EAME Campaign Medal with four Bronze Service Stars, one Bronze Arrowhead, the Good Conduct Medal, and the World War II Victory Medal. (Courtesy of Mrs. Eris S. Allen.)

Pvt. James Horace Atchley, 15th Air Force, entered the service on January 11, 1943, and received aircraft maintenance training in Georgia and California. Pvt. Horace Atchley and Pfc. Hubert Atchley, sons of Mr. and Mrs. J.R. Atchely of Rutherfordton, spent some time together in Italy. (Courtesy of Elizabeth A. Harrison.)

Pfc. Hubert Atchley received his overseas assignment to Oran, Algeria; subsequently he went to Sicily and Naples. His assignment in Naples was to the 1st Replacement Depot. A "Repple Depple Depot" was where replacements would arrive from the United States for assignment to their new units. It was in Italy that he was able to spend some time with his brother Pvt. James Horace Atchley. (Courtesy of Elizabeth A. Harrison.)

Six

CBI, Central Pacific Islands, D-Day, Philippine Islands, Battle of the Bulge (1944, 1945)

The U.S. Army and Navy in 1944 were advancing across the vast stretch of the Pacific and driving the Japanese toward their home islands. In that same year Gen. Douglas MacArthur made good his promise to return to the Philippines. In the European Theater, years of training and preparation achieved culmination with the massive invasion of Normandy. After breaking out of the beachheads, Allied forces pursued the remnants of the defeated German Army back to the borders of the Fatherland. Regrouping, the Nazis staged a last, desperate, and ultimately futile counterattack: the Ardennes Offensive.

Pfc. Baxter Waldon Guffey, USMC, participated in action at Kwajalein Atoll, Marshall Islands, between February 3 and February 8, 1944. Private Guffey served as a light anti-aircraft fire control man. He received an honorable discharge from the Marines on November 27, 1945. (Courtesy of Valoree Harrill.)

T/4 Max Sisk served with the 761st Engineer Light Equipment Company. Technician Sisk and his 300 fellow soldiers cleared land and set up base camps using bulldozers, motor graders, and other equipment on Eniwetok, Marshall Islands. Also serving in the Pacific was one of the five Carver brothers: Charlie Carver. Charlie's brother Gilford was with the Marine Corps at Camp Lejeune, North Carolina. (Courtesy of Max Sisk.)

T/5 P.D. Pilgrim, left, was in the 865th AAA AW Battalion; he served in the Western Pacific and earned the American Theater Campaign Medal, the Asiatic-Pacific Campaign Medal with one Bronze Service Star, the World War II Victory Medal, and the Good Conduct Medal. Homer Pilgrim, middle, served at the Naval Air Station in Pensacola, Florida; his rank was Aviation Machinist's Mate 1/C. T/5 J.V. Pilgrim, right, was in the Army and served in the Eastern Mandates with the 176th Station Hospital. He received the American Theater Campaign Medal, the Asiatic-Pacific Campaign Medal with one Bronze Service Star, the World War II Victory Medal, and the Good Conduct Medal. (Courtesy of Mary Frances Pilgrim.)

S/Sgt. George Clemmer Thomas served in Squadron 8/903rd Signal Platoon/Middle East Air Depot/IX Air Service Command. His unit served in India and issued both airborne and ground radio equipment and parts. He supervised 50 enlisted men and over 100 native laborers. He received the EAME Campaign Medal, Asiatic-Pacific Campaign Medal, and the Good Conduct Medal. (Courtesy of Lucy Earls.)

One of the seven McKinney brothers from Rutherford County to serve, Sgt. John C. McKinney began his career with Battery C/4th Field Artillery Battalion (Pack) at Fort Bragg. For six years he led mules in Fort Bragg before assuming the same duty in the CBI; he spent 14 months with the Nationalist Chinese Army. His most significant assignment was to the Old Guard, part of the 3rd Division, as Caisson Platoon Leader, in 1959. The Caisson Platoon carries a man to his final resting place at Arlington National Cemetery. He participated in the funerals of Presidents Hoover, Kennedy, Eisenhower, and Johnson. He retired in 1974 as a Chief Warrant Officer Four. (Courtesy of Pauline L. McKinney.)

T/4 John W. Tedder served in the 748th Railway Operating Battalion. Technician Tedder sailed 31 days from Los Angeles to Karachi and crossed Northern India to Calcutta. His next stop was Tinsukia, Assam, in Northeast India. John was an engineer on the Bengal-Assam Railroad in the Brahmaputra River Valley. The steam-powered, meter-gauge train brought troops, munitions, supplies, food, fuel, and mules in four-wheeled wagons from Mariani to Tinsukia, the railhead of the Ledo Road. Less than half of the 748th Railway Operating Battalion returned home. The photo depicts John, right, with a Naga tribesman. (Courtesy of John W. Tedder.)

While serving in India and Burma, T/4 William H. McArthur was a member of Company C/330th Engineer Battalion that built bridges and roads using all sorts of heavy equipment. They also constructed a gas pipeline to China. The U.S. used locals to assist in the construction and development work. (Courtesy of William H. McArthur.)

Here Bill McArthur is far from home and riding an Indian elephant, used as a beast of burden. The combatants in the Southeast Asia Theater prized elephants highly. Health was a constant concern; troops had to take medication regularly to prevent outbreaks of yellow fever and malaria spread by mosquitoes. For each man wounded in combat, 100 fell victim to disease. (Courtesy of William H. McArthur.)

T/Sgt. Robert L. Proctor served as supervisor and director of a section of the Stilwell Road/Ledo Road Headquarters in the CBI Theater. He served from November 25, 1941, to September 11, 1945. (Courtesy of Bea. H. Proctor.)

S/Sgt. Nathan A. Camby served with Company C/475th Infantry Regiment/5307th Composite Unit (Provisional) in Burma. A veteran of five battles, Sergeant Camby was a member of the volunteer unit Merrill's Marauders, which won the Presidential Citation for its exploits behind Japanese lines in Burma. Camby participated in the 700-mile trek through the Burma jungles; the Marauders surprised the enemy and dispatched 800 of them with a loss of only 4 Marauders. He received the Combat Infantryman's Badge (CIB) and other medals. (Courtesy of Margaret Camby.)

Pfc. John C. Morehead, 1712th Signal Service Battalion (AVA)/14th Air Force, served as a telephone operator. His most vivid memory was dining with Generalissimo Chiang Kai-Shek, Chinese Nationalist leader. An electric train carried food to the dinner table. Private Morehead received the Asiatic-Pacific Campaign Medal with one Bronze Service Star, the Good Conduct Medal, and the World War II Victory Medal. (Courtesy of Margaret P. Morehead.)

June 1944 brought the invasion of Guam Island, located in the Mariana Islands. In July came the invasions of the nearby islands Saipan and Tinian. Marine Pfc. Earl L. Curtis, Field Artillery, participated in the invasion of Guam and served also in the Philippines. His fellow Marines called him "Pop" because he was 29 years of age, and many of them were only 18 or 19 years old. (Courtesy of Jerry C. Camp.)

The operations on Guam included both the Marines and the Army. Pfc. Perry Elijah Whisnant served as a cook with Battery C/164th Field Artillery Battalion. While on Guam, he was in a foxhole when a Japanese grenade rolled in beside him. The grenade did not explode, and he brought it home as a souvenir. (Courtesy of Hilda H. Whisnant.)

Also serving in the Pacific was Pfc. Perry Whisnant's brother Pfc. Forrest W. Whisnant, left, a cartographer in the Army Air Forces. Another brother, Pvt. Carl Whisnant, right, was in the Army in Italy. (Both photos courtesy of Jim Brown, *Daily Courier*, and Hilda H. Whisnant.)

Pfc. Claude W. Brooks, Company A/305th Infantry Regiment/77th Division, served as an infantryman during combat on Guam Island, the Philippines, Okinawa, and later in the occupation of Japan. Private Brooks used a flamethrower to clear caves, bunkers, and pillboxes. "The Japanese wouldn't surrender, and we had to kill them." On Guam, in particular, a Japanese soldier attacked him with a bayonet secured on a bamboo pole. He also remembers the banzai charges at night. Brooks received the CIB, two Bronze Stars, the Purple Heart, and other medals. (Courtesy of Claude Brooks.)

First Sergeant Charles Madison Robbins, U.S. Army, Field Artillery/77th Division, participated in operations on Guam Island and Okinawa and in the occupation of Japan. Sergeant Robbins was the son of Mr. and Mrs. J.M. Robbins and husband of Edith Hunt Robbins.

The most famous operation of the European Theater was the invasion of Normandy on June 6, 1944: D-Day. This operation allowed the Allies to gain lodgment in Northwestern France and permitted a massive buildup of men and materials. Pfc. James B. Crow, Company I/3rd Battalion/18th Infantry Regiment/1st Division, was in the first wave on Omaha Beach. He recalls with pride how his platoon leader, 2nd Lt. Arthur Geers, when promoted to First Lieutenant, asked Private Crow to pin the silver bar on his uniform. Private Crow earned the CIB and four Bronze Service Stars for his campaigns in Sicily, Normandy, Northern France, the Rhineland. (Courtesy of James Broadus Crow.)

SP/4 Clyde Joe Stallings participated in all the major campaigns of the lst Division. Stallings describes the unit as beginning "like little boys playing in the sand, but by the end of the war, the Germans had learned to fear us." Stallings remembers Sicily: "A nasty country but good people who could sing like mockingbirds." In 1944 Field Marshall Montgomery addressed the 1st Division; Stallings remembers Montgomery asking the men to remove their helmets so he could see their faces. (Courtesy of Clyde J. Stallings.)

Pfc. Bobo Scruggs Sr., 121st Combat Engineer Company/29th Division, disembarked on Omaha Beach with the third wave. He remembers over 50 percent casualties. On July 10, 1944, Private Scruggs lost his left leg below the knee when a German tank fired on his jeep. He received rehabilitation at Lawson General Hospital in Atlanta; he was in traction for six months and had gangrene. His unit received the Presidential Unit Citation. (Courtesy of Bobo Scruggs Sr.)

Pfc. Warren Lodge Parker, Company A 119th Infantry Regiment/30th Division, remembers the "somber" trip to France for his first combat in Operation Cobra. The German resistance was "entrenched, and waiting for us . . . and [were] trying to annihilate us." Inland, "a German sniper with a silencer mowed me down [on August 28, 1944]. I was severely wounded, shot in the neck, back and leg." He lay unconscious overnight in a foxhole. Parker earned the Purple Heart, the CIB, the EAME Campaign Medal with one Bronze Service Star, the Good Conduct Medal, and the American Theater Medal. (Courtesy of Mabel Parker.)

(*below, left*) T/4 Arthur B. Bradley, below left, 278th Port Company, enlisted on April 26, 1943, and served until January 1, 1945. He served as a crane operator in Normandy and Northern France, earning the EAME Campaign Medal with two Bronze Service Stars, one Bronze Arrowhead, the World War II Victory Medal, and the Good Conduct Medal. (Courtesy of Judy Bradley.) (*below, right*) Also serving from Rutherford County in World War II was Frank Grayson. Grayson served in the Army.

T/4 Torrance Preston White, Company B/634th Tank Destroyer Battalion, took part in the initial breakout in the Carentan area, south of St. Lo. White's unit followed the drive to the German border and took part in operations on the Siegfried Line near Aachen. When they arrived at the Siegfried Line, the Germans began "firing more artillery and mortars than the book allowed." White was killed on March 30, 1945, by a German mortar. His grave marker at Margraten, Holland, reads, "T.P. White who gave his life for his country." (Courtesy of Liza Owens.)

Pfc. Howard A. Melton, Company C/33rd Armored Engineer Battalion, recalls how his unit preceded the main body in the push across France. Private Melton suffered shrapnel wounds on his right foot on September 27, 1944. He received the EAME Campaign Medal with five Bronze Stars and the Purple Heart; his battalion earned the Distinguished Unit Badge. (Courtesy of Howard A. Melton.)

Glenn McKinney, Company B/172nd Combat Engineer Battalion, served in Northern France, the Ardennes, and the Rhineland. With his musical talents he often assisted the chaplains in their divine services. McKinney served with Cpl. Arthur F. Price, who died before crossing "the last bridge" that he wrote home about. More information on Corporal Price is available on page 153 in *Real Heroes*. Nell Daves Price (Arthur's wife) and Lois McKinney traveled to Camp Breckinridge to visit with their husbands before their deployment overseas; co-author Anita Price Davis, five months old, slept on a pillow between their cots in the room the five of them shared. (Courtesy of Gertrude Silver.)

Pfc. Clyde M. Baldwin, 821st Military Police Company/3rd Army, served as a Military Policeman during operations in Northern France, the Ardennes, and Central Europe. (Courtesy of Hilda H. Whisnant.)

Cpl. John Glover Pruette, Company A/4th Engineer Combat Battalion, went ashore at Utah Beach. Upon landing in France, Pruette "ripped off his Corporal stripes and announced that he did not want to be responsible for the lives of other soldiers," according to wife Eva B. Pruette. Private Pruette was a foreman for the construction of roads and bridges. On November 17, 1944, during combat in the Hurtgen Forest, he received shrapnel wounds while on a mine-detecting mission. He was treated in England and sailed on the *Queen Mary* for further treatment in Texas. (Courtesy of Eva B. Pruette.)

(*below, left*) Pfc. George H. Wilson, 158th Ordnance Tire Repair Company, was a supply clerk. His unit oversaw the maintenance of tires on supply vehicles. He received the EAME Campaign Medal with four Bronze Service Stars, the Good Conduct Medal, and the World War II Victory Medal. (Courtesy of Hilda N. Wilson.) (*below, right*) S/Sgt. Jake Price, 82nd Adrm. Med. Sec., served from October 13, 1941 through September 7, 1945. He served in England, France, and Luxembourg. (Courtesy of Lorena V. Price.)

Cpl. Robert Maurice Sane, 9th Engineer Regiment, landed with the second wave on Omaha Beach and participated in the campaign for Northern France, the Ardennes, the Rhineland, and Central Europe. Corporal Sane earned the Purple Heart, the EAME Campaign Medal with five Bronze Service Stars, the Good Conduct Medal, and the World War II Victory Medal. (Courtesy of Robert Maurice Sane.)

Second Lieutenant John Sumner Smith, 29th Infantry Regiment, received his release from active duty on June 30, 1941. Recalled after the Japanese attack, Sumner served as company commander in the 501st Parachute Infantry Regiment. In April 1943 he received a transfer to Eastern Base Section at Watford, England, and Reims, France. He later went to Nancy, France, as personnel officer for the 10th Military Labor Service; he was in charge of 50,000 prisoners' records. He remained with the 10th Military Labor Service until the end of the war. Smith retired as a Lieutenant Colonel in 1968. (Courtesy of Martha Morris Estes.)

Cpl. George M. Tate, left, Company A/1258th Engineer Combat Battalion, drove trucks in England, France, Belgium, and Germany. Tate earned the EAME Campaign Medal with three Bronze Service Stars, the Good Conduct Medal, and the World War II Victory Medal. (Courtesy of George M. Tate.) Sgt. George E. Rhodes, right, Battery C/438th AAA AVN Battalion, served in Normandy, Northern France, the Ardennes, the Rhineland, and Central Europe. Sergeant Rhodes received five Bronze Service Stars on his EAME Campaign Medal. (Courtesy of Lillie Rhodes.)

First Lieutenant Tharo B. Godfrey, 13th Field Artillery Observation Battalion, enlisted in 1939 and received promotion in 1942 to Chief Warrant Officer. His unit landed at Utah Beach on D+4. He served in Normandy, Northern France, the Ardennes, the Rhineland, and Central Europe. He received a Bronze Star Medal and a battlefield commission to Second Lieutenant for meritorious service on April 24, 1945; three months later he received a promotion to First Lieutenant. Godfrey received the EAME Campaign Medal with five Bronze Service Stars. (Courtesy of T.B. Godfrey.)

T/4 George Thomas Carver, 117th General Hospital, was a surgical technician in England. Carver received the American Theater Service Medal, the EAME Campaign Medal, the Good Conduct Medal, and the World War II Victory Medal. His discharge came on February 23, 1946. (Courtesy of Juanita H. Carver.)

(*below, left*) T/5 George B. Whitaker, Company C/47th Engineer Construction Battalion, was one of five brothers serving in the Army during World War II. George served as a washing machine operator during the campaign across Northern France. (*below, right*) His brother Pvt. Paul G. Whitaker, Company C/540th Military Police Battalion, served during the postwar occupation of Germany. (Courtesy of Ruth Whitaker.)

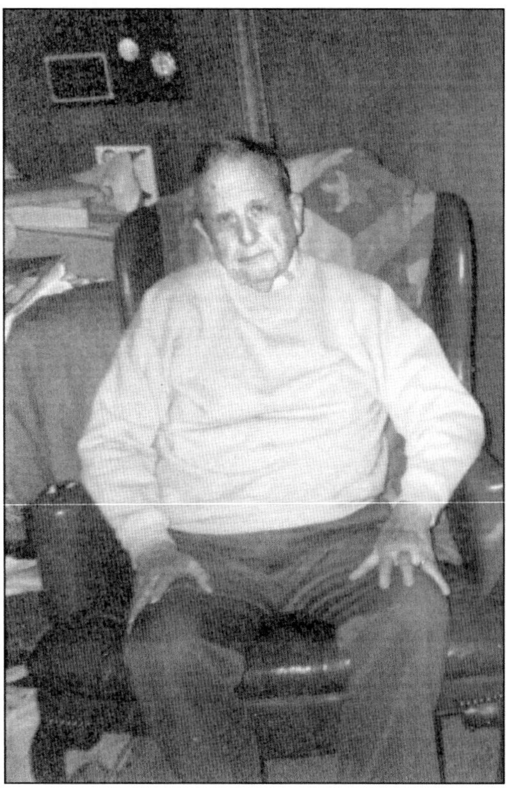

(*above, left*) During Normandy, Northern France, the Ardennes, the Rhineland, and Central Europe, Pfc. Melvin James Frazier, Battery C/219th Field Artillery Battalion/75th Division, drove supply trucks and received cross training as a cannoneer. (Courtesy of Johnny A. Frazier.) (*above, right*) Pfc. Joseph Dwight Hollifield died in France on July 4, 1944. His family has some poignant photos of him the day before he entered service, posed with his bulldog, Gary, in front of his home on Hollifield Road. (Courtesy of Kent Dorsey and Nell Melton Dorsey.)

Sgt. Hollis M. Owens Jr., Weapons Platoon/ Company E/104th Infantry Regiment 26th Division, served in Northern France, the Ardennes, and the Rhineland. On November 19, 1944, Sergeant Owens received wounds from artillery fire. Owens recalls talking with a fellow wounded soldier throughout the night until the man expired. Sergeant Owens received the Purple Heart, the CIB, the EAME Campaign Medal with three Bronze Service Stars, and the Good Conduct Medal. (Courtesy of Hollis M. Owens and Andrew John Robert Guttay.)

Pfc. Merrill S. York, Company C/110th Infantry Regiment/28th Division, served as squad leader during the Normandy, Northern France, and Ardennes campaigns. German troops captured Private York on December 19, 1944, during the Battle of the Bulge. Private York did not receive his freedom until April 25, 1945. (Courtesy of Madeline D. York Kendrick.)

Pfc. Merrill S. York's commendations include the EAME Campaign Medal, the three Bronze Service Stars, the Purple Heart, Good Conduct Medal, and the CIB. After his return to the United States, York married Madeline Daves on June 30, 1945. Here the happy couple relaxes outside Mount Vernon High School. (Courtesy of Madeline D. York Kendrick.)

Capt. Fred A. Wilkie, 18th Ordnance Bomb Disposal Squadron, commanded a bomb disposal unit. He diagnosed the type of unexploded bomb and determined the method of handling to avoid or minimize damage; he trained and instructed the unit in the use and maintenance of equipment and in the supply, transportation, and security of said items. In addition he investigated cases that were to come to trial, did summary court work, interviewed all men who received trial, and made recommendations to the review section for clemency or no clemency. (Courtesy of H.G. Wilkie.)

After unloading the cargo, the Landing Ship Tanks (LSTs) would be reconfigured to evacuate the wounded to hospitals in England. S1/C William Keller served as a crewman on the LST 55, which often carried the wounded. Keller still recalls "the stoic behavior in the face of mortal wounds as the young men were evacuated." (Courtesy of William Keller.)

T/4 Ralph J. Bridges, 297th General Hospital, served as a cook for over 500 men. Technician Bridges and his staff also helped transfer wounded to the hospitals in England. Doctors, 105 nurses, and 500 enlisted men served the needs of the sick, injured, and wounded. The hospital was under the overall command of Col. Francis J. Pruett. This Rutherford County native enjoyed his nickname of "Hillbilly." (Courtesy of Ralph J. Bridges.)

October 1944 brought the Central Pacific Offensive and the drive from the Southwestern Pacific Area together for the liberation of the Philippine Islands. S/S Britton H. Hayes, Company D/323rd Regiment/81st Division, was a squad leader in the liberation of the Philippines. After 18 months overseas, he returned home in January 1946. His son Douglas Hayes recalls that his father hated fireworks and beaches after his service. He remembers hearing his father say, "I've seen enough beaches and heard enough explosions to last a lifetime." (Courtesy of Douglas Hayes.)

Erma Lee Melton, wife of T/5 Herman Daniel Melton, 4613th Quartermaster Truck Company/508th Quartermaster Battalion, recalled that her husband, while in the Philippines, was a truck driver carrying supplies to the front. Technician Melton suffered wounds when a tank exploded. He received the Purple Heart, the American Campaign Medal, the Asiatic-Pacific Campaign Medal, and the Philippine Liberation Medal. (Courtesy of Erma Lee Melton.)

Cpl. James Elmer Branch, Battery C/304th Field Artillery/77th Division, served as a cannoneer who set the fuze for the artillery pieces. He received the Asiatic-Pacific Campaign Medal with four Bronze Service Stars, two American Defense Service Medals, the World War II Victory Medal, and the Good Conduct Medal. After the war, he became a minister. (Courtesy of Polly Branch.)

Eugene Carl Moore, U.S. Navy, served in the liberation of the Philippines. For his services, Moore received the Asiatic-Pacific Campaign Medal, the Philippine Liberation Medal, and the World War II Victory Medal. (Courtesy of Hilda Proctor.)

T/5 Grayson E. Johnston was a radio operator who moved with his unit from Zamboanga, Mindanao, Philippines, to Japan for occupation duty. While in Japan, Grayson and three of his buddies traveled to Hiroshima about five months after the atomic blast. "As far as the eye could see it was complete devastation," he recalled. (Courtesy of Sara Blanton Johnston.)

Pfc. Carl R. Baynard, Troop D/5th Cavalry Brigade/1st Cavalry Division, served as a cook during the liberation of Luzon Island. Private Baynard received the Asiatic-Pacific Campaign Medal with one Bronze Service Star, the Philippine Liberation Medal with one Bronze Service Star, the Good Conduct Medal, and the World War II Victory Medal. (Courtesy of Carl R. Baynard.)

T/5 Moses Dan Scruggs, Headquarters Troop/2nd Cavalry Brigade/1st Cavalry Division, was originally a combat engineer. During his time in the cavalry, he drove a truck and on occasion drove high-ranking officers. He saw service in New Guinea, the Bismarck Archipelago, the Southern Philippines, and Luzon Island. Dan earned the CIB, Asiatic-Pacific Campaign Medal with four Bronze Service Stars, the Philippine Liberation Medal, and the Good Conduct Medal. (Courtesy of Moses Dan Scruggs.)

T/5 Weldon Faye Hamrick, Headquarters Company/3rd Battalion/151st Infantry Regiment/38th Division, drove a 2-and-a-half-ton truck that transported food, ammunition, and supplies, and evacuated wounded to the rear. Technician Hamrick earned the CIB for service on Leyte Island at Zigzag Pass and Purple Heart Hill and the liberation of Bataan. Hamrick said, "The few Japanese who surrendered were nothing but skin and bones and were wearing nothing but loincloths." He concluded by saying, "I was nothing but a country boy who found it all overwhelming." (Courtesy of Weldon Faye Hamrick.)

T/5 William Glenn Murray was a cook in the 182nd Infantry Regiment/37th Division during operations in the Southern Philippines. He earned the Asiatic-Pacific Campaign Medal with one Bronze Service Star, the Philippine Liberation Medal with one Bronze Star, the World War II Victory Medal, and the Good Conduct Medal. (Courtesy of Christa Ingle.)

Pfc. John T. Harris, third from left, Company A/182nd Field Artillery Battalion, served in a 4.2-inch mortar battery. He relates how troops shared food with starving Filipinos. While serving in Yokohoma, Private Harris remembers how calm people were, how children would give the Victory sign, and how they would greet Americans with, "Hello, Joe." Private Harris visited Hiroshima where "the sand was blasted black and was smooth as glass." His most vivid memory of the war was leaving his wife and five children. (Courtesy of John T. Harris.)

T/5 William Francis Goode, Company B/718th Amphibious Tractor Battalion attached to the 7th Division, drove an amphibious tractor. He saw service in the Southern Philippines and at Luzon and Okinawa. He received the American Campaign Service Medal, the Asiatic-Pacific Campaign Medal with two Bronze Service Stars, one Bronze Arrowhead, and the Philippine Liberation Medal with two Bronze Service Stars. His best memory of World War II was when President Truman dropped the A-bomb and "I would not have to invade Japan." He also recalled the death of 10th Army Commander Lt. Gen. Simon Bolivar Buckner on June 18, 1945. (Courtesy of William Francis Goode.)

T/4 William C. "Bill" Hightower, 3437th Ordnance Company, was in a unit responsible for the replacement, repair, and rebuilding of tanks, guns, trucks, rifles, and machine guns. From their base at Guadalcanal, these men forwarded the repaired materials to the Philippines. Technician Hightower recalls vividly the explosion and sinking of the USS *Serpens* by a two-man midget Japanese submarine on January 25, 1945. He received the Asiatic-Pacific Campaign Medal, the World War II Victory Medal, and the Good Conduct Medal. (Courtesy of Bill Hightower.)

T/4 Henry L. Whitaker, Headquarters Company 551st Signal Air Warning Battalion, served during operations to liberate the Philippine Islands. He was a heavy-truck driver for the unit. He received the American Theater Service Medal, the Asiatic-Pacific Campaign Medal, the World War II Victory Medal, and the Good Conduct Medal. (Courtesy of Ruth Whitaker.)

Lt. Col. Charles William Biggerstaff served as Stevedore Officer in command of the 388th Port Battalion and the 492nd Port Battalion. Colonel Biggerstaff, as commanding officer, was responsible for the movement of supplies to the troops on the front. His stations included New Caledonia, the Russell Islands, Guadalcanal, and the Philippines. He also served during the occupation of Japan at Yokohoma. (Courtesy of Virginia B. Rucker.)

Pfc. William Alton Tate, Battery D/382nd AAA AW Battalion, served in the Pacific. He received his induction into the service on October 5, 1942, and his training at Camp Wallace, Texas; Camp Hulen, Texas; and at a desert training center in California. (Courtesy of Mrs. Delvo Scruggs.)

T/Sgt. James D. Culbertson, 124th Combat Ordnance Company/3rd Army, was responsible for small arms maintenance and repair. He recalls going out on "road patrols" to retrieve abandoned equipment. His most vivid memory is the scene of a German atrocity: Germans had locked a huge number of French civilians in a barn and set fire to it. Culbertson saw service in France, Belgium, Luxembourg, and Germany. His poem "The Army Life" appears on page 2 of this volume. (Courtesy of James D. Culbertson.)

(*below, left*) Pvt. Jesse L. Johnson, 2128th Army Air Force Base Unit, served in Europe from October 1942 until February 1945. (*below, right*) His brother T/5 Henry Baxter Johnson, of the 79th and 698th Field Artillery Battalions served between March 1941 and October 1945. These are two of the five Johnson brothers who served in World War II; their father was John Franklin Johnson Sr. of Rutherford County. (Courtesy of James Johnson Jr.)

T/5 John Franklin Johnson Jr., left, Headquarters Company/48th Tank Battalion, served between May 1943 and January 1946. S/Sgt. David Coy Johnson, right, 99th Infantry Division, served from November 25, 1942, until his death in action on March 15, 1945, in Germany. Complete details on David Coy Johnson are in *Real Heroes*. These are two more of the five Johnson brothers who served in World War II. (Courtesy of James Johnson Jr.)

Sgt. James Johnson, 705th Air Materials Squadron/463rd Air Service Group, attached to the 83rd Infantry Division, participated in the Ardennes, the Rhineland, and the Central Europe Campaigns. Sergeant Johnson received two Purple Hearts and the EAME Campaign Medal with Bronze Service Star. He was one of five Johnson brothers who served in World War II. (Courtesy of James Johnson Jr.)

Pfc. Boyce L. Ingle, Company I/314th Infantry Regiment/79th Division, participated in the Battle of Hurtgen Forest. He served also in the Ardennes, the Rhineland, and the Central Europe Campaigns. He won the CIB, the EAME Campaign Medal with three Bronze Service Stars, and the Good Conduct Medal. (Courtesy of Geneva Ingle.)

Cpl. William A. "Gus" Rich, 116th Ordnance Medium Maintenance Company/3rd Army, served in the European Theater from January 8, 1945, until the end of the war. He and his unit participated in the Ardennes, the Rhineland, and the Central Europe campaigns. He earned the EAME Campaign Medal with three Bronze Service Stars and the World War II Victory Medal. (Courtesy of Charles E. Rich.)

T/5 James E. Kirby, Battery C/796th AAA (SP)/3rd Army, manned a quad .50 caliber anti-aircraft gun that fired 2,800 rounds per minute and took two cannoneers to keep loaded. He served in the Ardennes, the Rhineland, and Central Europe and won the Bronze Star Medal, the American Theater Campaign Medal, the EAME Campaign Medal with three Bronze Service Stars, the Good Conduct Medal, and the World War II Victory Medal. (Courtesy of James E. Kirby.)

(*below, left*) Pvt. Glenn H. Robbins Sr., 393rd Infantry Regiment/99th Division, participated in Normandy, Northern France, and the Ardennes. Private Robbins suffered wounds at the Battle of the Bulge; he earned the Purple Heart, the CIB, the EAME Campaign Medal with three Bronze Service Stars, and the Good Conduct Medal. (Courtesy of Glenn H. Robbins Sr.) (*below, right*) Pfc. James Womack, 670th Bombardment Squadron, drove trucks in Normandy, Northern France, the Ardennes, the Rhineland, and Central Europe and earned the Purple Heart, the EAME Campaign Medal with six Bronze Service Stars, and the Good Conduct Medal. (Courtesy of James Womack.)

T/4 Bynum G. Norville, left, Company C/17th Tank Battalion/7th Armored Division, drove tanks in Northern France, the Ardennes, the Rhineland, and Central Europe. He served two years, three months, and six days. He received the Purple Heart, the Bronze Star Medal, the EAME Campaign Medal with four Bronze Service Stars, and the Good Conduct Medal. The photo shows Bynum Norville and fellow Rutherford County resident Fred McCurry, right. (Courtesy of Lucille Clements.)

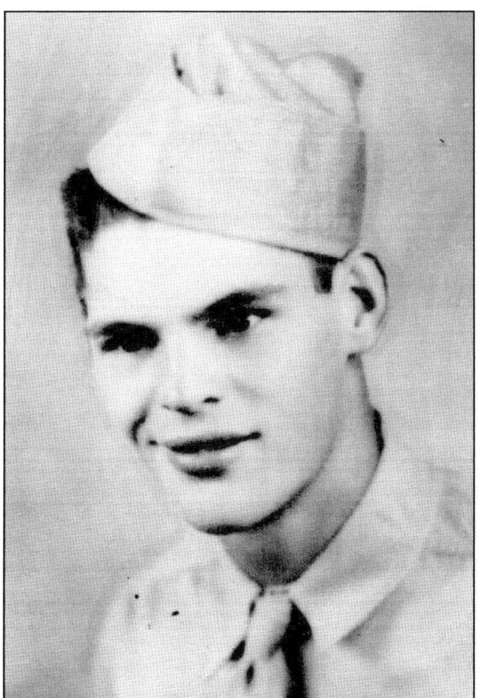

T/5 Harold G. Keever was in Company C/61st Armored Infantry 10th Armored Division. Odean Keever, his son, says his father never talked much about his service, but he did tell his wife about being trapped behind German lines during the Battle of the Bulge. A French family that spoke no English hid him for nine days during Christmas 1944. He won the Purple Heart, CIB, the EAME Campaign Medal with three Bronze Service Stars, and the Good Conduct Medal. (Courtesy of Odean Keever.)

Pfc. Charles R. Miller, Company A/10th Infantry Regiment/5th Division, served in Northern France, the Ardennes, and the Rhineland. He became a POW on January 28, 1945. His confinement in German Stalag XIIA lasted until British tanks freed him on April 16, 1945. Miller said, "They liked to starved us to death." Miller earned the Bronze Star Medal, the EAME Campaign Medal with three Bronze Service Stars, the Good Conduct Medal, and the World War II Victory Medal. (Courtesy of Charles R. Miller.)

T/5 Robert Charles Condrey, 14th Field Artillery/2nd Armored Division, drove a half-track mounting a 105mm howitzer. Technician Condrey recalls Sicily, going ashore at Normandy on D+5, the St. Lo bombardment, and the knee-deep snow of the Battle of the Bulge. He remembers how German artillery killed his best friend in a foxhole. Technician Condrey served from 1940 through the end of the war; he was at Fort Benning, Georgia, the day of Pearl Harbor. (Courtesy of Robert Charles Condrey.)

T/5 Joel Ralph Morrow was in Headquarters Company/91st Chemical Mortar Battalion. He found a small dog and took care of it all during World War II. Ralph was a truck driver responsible for the transportation of the mortar and its crewmen. He served in the Ardennes, the Rhineland, and Central Europe and received the EAME Campaign Medal, the Good Conduct Medal, and the World War II Victory Medal. (Courtesy of Janice Morrow.)

T/4 Thomas L. Porter Sr. served in the 804th Military Police Company in Northern France. As a military police officer, he enforced military laws and regulations and helped protect civilians and military personnel in combat areas. He earned the American Theater Service Medal, the EAME Campaign Medal with one Bronze Service Stars, the World War II Victory Medal, and the Good Conduct Medal. (Courtesy of Thomas L. Porter.)

Joe D. Aldrich, left, served in the Army. He earned the Bronze Star Medal, American Theater Campaign Medal, the EAME Campaign Medal with four Bronze Service Stars, the World War II Victory Medal, and the Good Conduct Medal. His brother Aviation Ordnance Mate 1/C Frank Lindsey Aldrich, right, served four years in the Navy. (Courtesy of Gertrude Aldrich Silver.)

Pvt. John B. Sane, Company B/15th Infantry Regiment/3rd Division, served during the reduction of the Colmar Pocket near Strasbourg, France. Serving with Sane was war hero Audie Murphy. More information on John B. Sane is in *Rutherford County in World War II: Volume I*, page 94. His brother Mack C. Sane was killed in action in Germany on April 4, 1945. More information on Mack Sane is on page 171 in *Real Heroes*. (Courtesy of Clara Sane.)

Seven

A Two-Ocean War (1941–1945)

Atlantic and Pacific

The naval battle in the Atlantic Ocean presented the Atlantic Fleet with the challenge of helping the Royal Navy to eliminate the German submarine menace. The defeat of the U-boats would allow the Allies to move both the vital supplies and the millions of troops necessary to ensure the defeat of Adolf Hitler across the sea. These sailors overcame the "wolf packs" and the fierce storms of the North Atlantic Ocean. The navy's success freed Europe from the grasp of the cruel tyrant. After the attack on Pearl Harbor, the Pacific Fleet faced the well-trained and hard-fighting Japanese Imperial Fleet. Ranging across the vast ocean were ships that spanned the entire inventory of the American Navy. Using every type of ship, from small landing craft to the far-ranging carrier task forces, the U.S. Navy battled the implacable foe. By September 1945, the fleet, under command of fighting admirals like William F. Halsey Jr., Raymond A. Spruance, and Marc A. Mitscher, had defeated the proud Japanese. With the surrender in Tokyo Bay, the U.S. Navy reached a pinnacle of power it has maintained until the present day.

Claude Carroll Robbins, U.S. Navy, enlisted on September 30, 1940, and advanced to chief machinist's mate. He received appointment to flight school, and upon completion of his pilot training, Ensign Robbins received assignment to VF 82 aboard the USS *Bennington*, which participated in the battles of Iwo Jima, Okinawa, and in aerial strikes against the home islands of Japan. Lieutenant (jg) Robbins flew a Grumman F6F Hellcat fighter. His brother Max trained naval aviators; his brother Clark also served. (Courtesy of Claude Carroll Robbins.)

Small ships and aircraft were the main components of the naval war in the Atlantic. Pfc. Hamlet Lemaster Harmon, 601st Military Police Battalion, received conditional discharge from the Coastal Artillery in November 1941. Recalled to active duty on January 8, 1942, he received his assignment to Port of Spain, Trinidad, where he guarded the vital oil fields for two years. Private Harmon completed his tour of duty at Camp Shelby, Mississippi. (Courtesy of Sandra H. Crawley.)

Cpl. Jack T. Newton was in the 858th Guard Patrol at Hamilton Air Force Base in Bermuda. For his services, Corporal Newton received the American Theater Service Medal with one Bronze Service Star, the Good Conduct Medal, and the World War II Victory Medal. (Courtesy of Jack T. Newton.)

Pharmacist's Mate 2/C Elaine Richards Hudson served as a nurse at Naval Air Station Corpus Christi, Texas. On October 25, 1944, she married Ross Hudson. Aviation Chief Machinist's Mate Arthur Ross Hudson, right, served in VP 83 and VPB 107 based out of Natal, Brazil. Chief Hudson's squadron attacked 25 submarines and received credit for 9 confirmed sub kills. The squadron received the Presidential Unit Citation for its role in the Battle of the Atlantic. (Courtesy of Elaine Richards Hudson.)

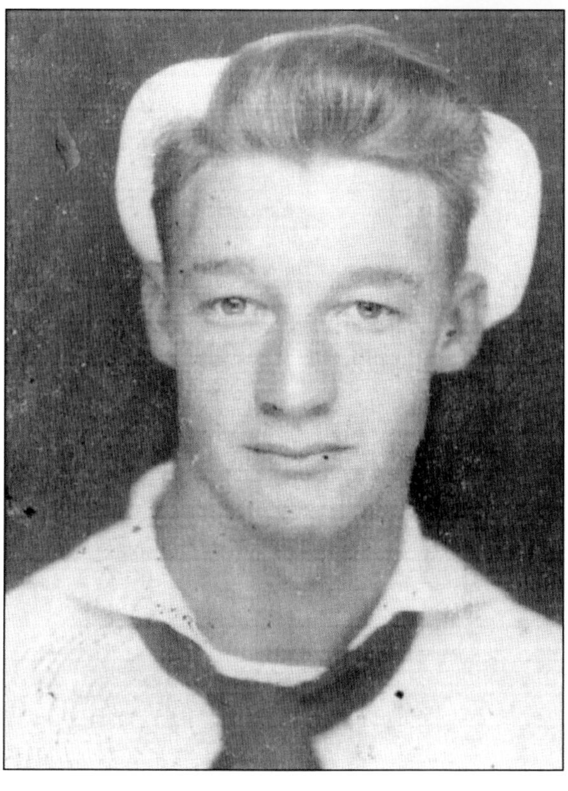

S/3C Junior M. Johnson served on the USS *Marsh*; the *Marsh* and other escorts protected the vital convoys that sailed from North America to Great Britain to deliver supplies and troops. The escorts were always on alert for the undersea threat. (Courtesy of Junior M. Johnson.)

(*above, left*) Machinist's Mate 3/C William Archie Hodge served on the USS *Marts*. The duties of the *Marts* included escorting aircraft carriers, countering the ever-present U-boats, and even sinking one or two of them. The *Marts*'s service was throughout the South Atlantic. (Courtesy of William Archie Hodge.) (*above, right*) Gunner's Mate 3/C John Henry Jenkins served on the USS *Gantner*. The *Gantner* escorted battleships; on May 10, 1944, she sank a German U-boat. (Courtesy of Geneva Jenkins.)

Torpedoman's Mate 2/C Barney Yates Hamrick served on the USS *Woolsey*. He and his fellow crewmen participated in the invasions of North Africa, Sicily, Anzio, and Southern France. The *Woolsey* received credit for sinking the *U-73*, rescuing 23 German survivors, and assisting in the sinking of the *U-960*. (Courtesy of Karen J. Dotson.)

S1/C Alton Evan Conner served as a coxswain of a 50-foot Landing Craft Mechanized (LCM) during Operation Dragoon, the invasion of Southern France, in August 1944. His brother Burl D. Conner served on board LST 505 in Europe. Here Burl, left, and Alton, right, pose together. (Courtesy of Alton Conner.)

Second Mate Warner W. Stewart, Squadron D/Group I, served as a deck officer on the *Caleb Strong*. The ship sailed from the United States to Great Britain, the Mediterranean, and the Soviet Union. Second Mate Stewart served from January 22, 1942, until December 2, 1945. (Courtesy of Warner W. Stewart.)

George Logan Lane served in the Merchant Marines aboard the *John Milledge*, which helped to transport troops and supplies to England. Lane was in the Army Air Forces postwar. He was with the 136th Army Airways Communication Squadron, based in Iceland. This photo shows George Logan Lane on the roof of a Quonset hut. (Courtesy of George Logan Lane.)

Wilbur J. Burgin served as a junior officer on the USS *Eugene A. Green* during operations in the Mediterranean Sea. After the war, Burgin "won his wings;" he served on several aircraft carriers: the *Independence*, the *Boxer*, and the *Shangri-La*, where he served as air boss. Burgin retired as Captain. (Courtesy of Wilbur J. Burgin.)

Among the most hazardous duties of the U.S. Navy was being a submariner. Chief Pharmacist's Mate Harold C. Lane served aboard the USS *Scamp* and the USS *Guardfish*. Chief Pharmacist's Mate Lane enlisted in October 1939. The submarines that he served aboard had bases in Australia and attacked Japanese shipping in waters off Southeast Asia. He transferred off the *Scamp* to the *Guardfish* just before the loss of the *Scamp* with all hands on November 9, 1944. (Courtesy of Harold C. Lane.)

Aviation Machinist's Mate 3/C Arthur W. Kendrick served in Hawaii and Johnson Island. He received the American Theater Medal, the Asiatic-Pacific Campaign Medal, and the World War II Victory Medal. (Courtesy of Madeline Daves York Kendrick.)

Arm/2C T. Lyles Mason served in VS 66 and VS 52 as a radio operator. While flying in a SB2C-4 Helldiver, he and his squadron conducted patrols from the Marshall Islands against the Japanese-held islands of Wotje and Jaluit. He was able to make it home by Christmas 1945. (Courtesy of T. Lyles Mason.)

Fireman 1/C John Drury Wilson served in both the Atlantic and Pacific aboard the Landing Craft Infantry (L) 821. Because of his hazardous duty, he received the American Theater Medal, the Asiatic-Pacific Campaign Medal, and the World War II Victory Medal. He served between 1943 and 1946. (Courtesy of Hilda N. Wilson.)

Cook 3/C Enos Logan served in California and Virginia for more than two years. He won the Asiatic-Pacific Campaign Medal and the World War II Victory Medal. (Courtesy of Enos Logan.)

Boatswain's Mate 1/C Vollie Sherman Dalton served aboard the USS *Burais*, a repair ship that was always near the front lines. He was one of the few who served during the entire era of World War II. He earned the Asiatic-Pacific Campaign Medal, the American Theater Medal, the World War II Victory Medal, and the Good Conduct Medal. (Courtesy of Vollie Sherman Dalton.)

S1/C Addie Joseph Smart served on the USS *San Saba*, an attack transport that carried soldiers or Marines to the invasion sites for loading into smaller landing craft for the assault on the beaches. He received the American Theater Medal, the Asiatic-Pacific Campaign Medal, the Philippine Liberation Medal, and the World War II Victory Medal. (Courtesy of Ruby Smart.)

Fireman 1/C Charles C. Hamrick served aboard the USS *Bollinger*, an attack transport. The ship supplied logistical support for the follow-up of the Iwo Jima invasion; they also carried cargo and passengers throughout the Central Pacific. Charles and his wife were sweethearts from the first grade! (Courtesy of Ruth Hamrick.)

S1/C Paul Grayson Dalton served on the USS *Rombach*, which escorted transport ships in the war zone. The *Rombach* destroyed 11 mines while he was on duty. After the surrender of Japan, the *Rombach* delivered mail to U.S. service personnel in Shanghai, China. Dalton was drafted although he had two sons at home. (Courtesy of Paul G. Dalton.)

S1/C John Baxter Harrill served aboard the USS *Raco* and the USS *Grout*. He was undergoing amphibious training for the invasion of Japan, Operation Olympic, when the war ended; he believed the invasion would have cost thousands of lives. He would always chuckle and say, "I came home on a magic carpet." (Photo and information courtesy of Valoree Harrill and Janet Harrill.)

S1/C Oral James Ferguson served as a gunner aboard the USS *Hancock*. The *Hancock* participated in the Philippine liberation, the invasion of Iwo Jima, and various Pacific raids. The *Hancock* received damage from an explosion on January 21, 1945, and by a Kamikaze plane on July 4, 1945. Ferguson received wounds during his tour of duty. He is in the second row, seventh from the left. (Courtesy of Christine Downey.)

S1/C Richard Baker "Bud" McFarland was a plank-owner (aboard at the commissioning of the ship) in the 7th Division of the crew of the USS *Pittsburgh*. During combat he served as a trainer on a quad 40mm anti-aircraft gun on the starboard side of the ship. He remembers the *Pittsburgh* towing the seriously damaged *Franklin*. He was aboard when a typhoon ripped the bow off the ship on June 5, 1945. He received his discharge in March 1946. (Courtesy of Bud McFarland.)

S2/C Charles Yates Lavender served on the USS *Pittsburgh* and he remembers the loss of the bow during the typhoon. The crew's skillful damage control saved the ship and after major repairs the *Pittsburgh* returned to combat. (Courtesy of Denise P. Gavin.) Also serving on the *Pittsburgh* were Eliot James Teseniar and Vaughn Hamrick; more information on them is available in *Rutherford County in World War II: Volume I*, page 108.

Lt. (jg) Richard Brucksch Jr. discovered an uncharted reef; it was to "be named after the discoverer, Ensign R. Brucksch, USNR Naval Air Base, Saipan. Ensign Richard Brucksch sighted this reef on 15 January 1945 while flying at an altitude of 500 feet and at a distance of approximately three miles." Brucksch served as third pilot of a PBY-5A of the VPB 23; because of the duration of the flights, one pilot could not serve for the entire mission. This unit flew search-and-rescue missions. This is the official patch of the VPB 23, courtesy of Richard Brucksch Jr.

Carpenter's Mate 3/C Louis Wade Sarratt served aboard the USS *Kangaroo*, a station oil tanker for fuel storage for the Pacific bases. Carpenter's Mate Sarratt remembered Okinawa and New Zealand as two base locations. He married his girl friend Virginia Dare Daggerhart. (Courtesy of his family.)

Before his induction into the Navy, Willie D. Hall was a ship fitter who constructed liberty ships at the Bethlehem Steel Shipyard in Baltimore, Maryland. Hall remembered the construction sites were so smoky, "you had to follow the welding cables from the ship's bottom." In late 1944 Hall was drafted into the Navy; Ship Fitter 2/C Willie D. Hall served aboard the USS *Menelaus*, an auxiliary repair ship based in Saipan. The photo is of Willie and Murleen Hall in the Union Township. (Courtesy of Willie Hall.)

(*above, left*) S2/C James Amos Cole, above left, served aboard the USS *New York* during Iwo Jima and Okinawa. "A dive bomber dove on the USS *New York* and James was in the crow's nest when the plane hit the ship. It caused damages that resulted in a return to Pearl Harbor for repairs." (Photo and information courtesy of Billy Seay.) (*above, right*) Petty Officer 2/C Wilburn Shirley Jolley, above right, served aboard the USS *Texas*, LST 446, and LST 1108. He earned the American Campaign Medal and the Asiatic-Pacific Campaign Medal. (Courtesy of Opal Jolley.)

Petty Officer 2/C Arbuth Durward Hamrick was aboard the USS *Sims* in both the Atlantic and the Pacific. For 17 months the *Sims* escorted convoys from Venezuela to Iceland to England. In 1944 the *Sims* received transfer to the Pacific, where Hamrick served in Engine Room 1. The *Sims* participated in Okinawa, during which time a kamikaze plane struck the ship; the attack resulted in a return to Saipan for repairs. (Courtesy of Mary Olga Watson Hamrick and Jelma Hamrick Daves.)

EMC Charles H. Walker served aboard the LCT 27 and took part in Normandy, Iwo Jima, and Okinawa, where he stayed for 93 days. He earned the EAME Campaign Medal with one Bronze Service Star, the Asiatic-Pacific Campaign Medal with two Bronze Service Stars, and the Philippine Liberation Medal. (Courtesy of Charles H. Walker.)

Fireman 1/C Claud Paul Goforth served aboard the USS *Texas*, at the invasion of Iwo Jima and Okinawa. His son William Buck Goforth, remembers that while he was serving aboard the USS *Briareus*, his cargo ship pulled alongside his father's battleship. The son asked to go aboard to visit his father, but the commander would not allow this because of an impending typhoon. When the two were finally able to meet, it was a very emotional reunion. (Courtesy of William Buck Goforth.)

S/1C James M. Biggerstaff served aboard the USS *Nevada* at Normandy and Southern France in 1944. In February 1945 the *Nevada* pounded Iwo Jima and finished its career at Okinawa when a Kamikaze struck. For his services Biggerstaff received the EAME Campaign Medal with two Bronze Service Stars, the Asiatic-Pacific Campaign Medal with two Bronze Service Stars, and the World War II Victory Medal. (Courtesy of Jim Biggerstaff.)

Radioman 3/C Donald H. Randall was a plank-owner of the USS *New Jersey*. The ship participated in the Marshall Islands, the Mariana Islands, Leyte Gulf, the Philippine liberation, Iwo Jima, Okinawa, and the surrender at Tokyo Bay. The *New Jersey* served as Adm. William F. Halsey's 3rd Fleet Flagship. Randall received the Asiatic-Pacific Campaign Medal with nine Bronze Service Stars, the Philippine Liberation Medal with two Bronze Service Stars, and the World War II Victory Medal. (Courtesy of Donald H. Randall.)

Chief Gunner's Mate Jacob Dexter Yelton Jr. was aboard the USS *California* on December 7, 1941. His response to the surprise attack was, "My God! It's the Japs!" Wounded by shrapnel and burned from hot fuel, he received the Purple Heart. Returning to active duty on the USS *Barton*, Yelton had to remain in the water for 14 hours when his ship was sunk at Guadalcanal on Friday, November 13, 1942. He became a plank-owner on the USS *Frankford* and participated in the invasion of Normandy. In August 1945, the *Frankford* was one of the first ships to enter the harbor of Hiroshima. For his six years of service, Chief Yelton received the Pearl Harbor Medal, the American Defense Service Medal with one Bronze Service Star, the American Area Campaign Medal, the EAME Campaign Medal with two Bronze Service Stars, the Asiatic-Pacific Campaign Medal, the World War II Victory Medal, and the Good Conduct Medal. The family stated that "J.D. was a true survivor, but he lost a three-year battle with cancer, September 9, 1986." (Courtesy of Ola Williams Yelton.)

Eight

Germany, Iwo Jima, and Okinawa (1945)

Prevailing in Europe and Battling in the Pacific

In the Pacific American forces readied themselves to attack Iwo Jima and Okinawa to open the way to the home islands of Japan. The year of 1945 began with the defeat of the last German counteroffensive in the west. In the east the Soviet Union's Red Army stood on the Oder River and made ready for the final attack on Berlin.

Cpl. Robert C. Watson, Medical Detachment/315th Infantry Regiment/79th Division, served in Normandy, Northern France, the Rhineland, and Central Europe. He suffered wounds in combat on October 10, 1944. Corporal Watson entered the service in January 1940 and received discharge in August 1945. He earned the Purple Heart, the American Defense Service Medal, and the EAME Campaign Medal with four Bronze Service Stars. (Courtesy of Pam Robinson, his daughter.)

Pfc. Roy Owensby is one of the few men from the county who served in both the Army and the Army Air Forces. While in the USAAF, Owensby was in Company B/318th Infantry Regiment/80th Division. Private Owensby earned the CIB, the American Theater Campaign Medal, the EAME Campaign Medal with three Bronze Service Stars, the Good Conduct Medal, and the World War II Victory Medal. He served in the Rhineland and Central Europe. (Courtesy of Betty Owensby Byers.)

James Guy Brooks enlisted in the Navy on July 20, 1943. His station was Alameda Naval Air Station in California. Three months after his discharge, he enlisted in the Army on June 27, 1946. He served as a private in Troop O/74th Construction Squadron in Germany. For his combined services, Brooks received the Asiatic-Pacific Campaign Medal, the EAME Campaign Medal, the World War II Victory Medal, and the Army of Occupation Medal. (Courtesy of Debbie Gosey.)

(*above, left*) S/Sgt. Garland Glenn Hamrick served in the 14th Armored Division, "the Liberators." During the winter of 1945, he remembers that there was no heat in the tanks or half-tracks and the snow was waist deep. His vehicle was hit by a German 88mm on January 12, 1945 and he lost one of his legs. Recovery and rehabilitation took one year at the Lawson General Hospital in Atlanta. (Courtesy of G.G. Hamrick.) (*above, right*) Pfc. Ralph Allen Humphries served in the Army as a Military Policeman. For his services he received the EAME Campaign Medal with one Bronze Service Star, the World War II Victory Medal, and the Good Conduct Medal. (Courtesy of Donald Ray Humphries.)

Cpl. Charles Monroe Hawkins, Battery C/798th AAA AW Battalion, remembers scrubbing the floor of the barracks with a toothbrush during basic training and uniforms in two sizes: too big or too little. Participating in the Rhineland and Central Europe, Hawkins was a cannoneer on his 40mm gun. He received the American Theater Service Medal, the EAME Campaign Medal with two Bronze Service Stars, and the World War II Victory Medal. (Courtesy of Charles M. Hawkins.)

T/5 Housan P. Harrill, 3705th Quartermaster Truck Company/1st Army, served as truck driver. He saw action in Normandy, Northern France, the Ardennes, the Rhineland, and Central Europe. Without the services of the quartermaster companies, the Allied advance across France to Germany could not have taken place successfully. The importance of the units was critical to the ultimate Allied success. (Courtesy of H.P. Harrill.)

Sgt. Billy B. Harrill, Battery B/554th AAA AW Battalion/94th Division, is a brother of H.P. Harrill. He served in Northern France, the Ardennes, the Rhineland, and Central Europe. He recalls going ashore that "he had never seen such destruction." He recalls a particular scene of horror: a retreating German unit and its horses destroyed by napalm and the resulting odor from the burned flesh of animals and humans. Among his many decorations is the EAME Campaign Medal with four Bronze Service Stars. (Courtesy of Billy B. Harrill.)

Pfc. Hubert Yelton, center, served with an infantry division that held and threw back the German advance on Belgium. Mrs. Yelton learned from 1st Lt. Robert F. Blume of her husband's "self-sacrifices. . . suffering. . . and the hardships he has sustained in protecting our way of life . . . It was his feats and those of men like him that will be discussed forever when men gather to talk of unsung heroes." Yelton received the CIB, the EAME Campaign Medal with three Bronze Service Stars, and the Good Conduct Medal. His brother Pvt. Clarence Yelton, left, and S2/C Johnnie Yelton, right, also served. (Photo and information courtesy of Eunice Yelton.)

Pfc. Charles E. Jackson Sr. served as a mail clerk in an infantry unit attached to the 7th Army. In a V-mail letter home Jackson expressed his remembrances and his concern for his loved ones. Mail kept up the morale of the men, particularly those at the front. For his services Private Jackson received the EAME Campaign Medal with two Bronze Service Stars, the Good Conduct Medal, and the World War II Victory Medal. (Photo and information courtesy of Frances Robbins.)

T/Sgt. Merrill D. Hampton, right, 1290th Engineer Combat Battalion 3rd Division 7th Army, served as a medic. He participated in the Rhineland and Central Germany. He earned the EAME Campaign Medal with two Bronze Service Stars and the World War II Victory Medal. The unit left from Germany in July 1945 and was told that it would participate in the invasion of Japan. "Two days out of port we received the news that Japan had surrendered." (Courtesy of Merrill D. Hampton.)

Pfc. Grover T. Smith, shown here in Germany, served in the infantry in the Rhineland and Central Europe. He received the EAME Campaign Medal with two Bronze Service Stars, the American Theater Campaign Medal, the Good Conduct Medal, and the World War II Victory Medal. (Courtesy of Grover T. Smith.)

(*above, left*) Pfc. Charlie Burgess, 276th Infantry Regiment/70th Division, served in Southern France and Germany. He earned the CIB, the EAME Campaign Medal, and the Good Conduct Medal. (Courtesy of Charlie Burgess.) (*above, right*) Pfc. Charles F. Greene, Battery A 665th Field Artillery Battalion, served in the Rhineland and Central Europe campaigns. His duty was that of a cannoneer; for his services he earned the EAME Campaign Medal with two Bronze Service Stars, the American Campaign Medal, the World War II Victory Medal, and the Good Conduct Medal. (Courtesy of Jeaul Greene.)

Pfc. Marcus D. Hyder, Company B 274th Infantry Regiment 70th Division, saw combat in the Rhineland and Central Europe. After V-E Day he received assignment to the 7th Infantry 3rd Division. He guarded POWs at Hersfeld, Germany, and assisted in the enforcement of rules and regulations of the Allied Armies. He earned the CIB, the EAME Campaign Medal with two Bronze Service Stars, the Good Conduct Medal, and the World War II Victory Medal. (Courtesy of Randy Hyder.)

Pfc. William Boyce Wilkerson, Company C/333rd Infantry Regiment/83rd Division, served in the Rhineland and Central Europe. He earned the CIB and suffered wounds from shrapnel in Germany in 1945. He often said, "the most beautiful sight was the Statue of Liberty on his way home." He also earned the American Service Medal, the EAME Campaign Medal with three Bronze Service Stars, the Good Conduct Medal, and the World War II Victory Medal. (Courtesy of Michelle Harris.) Earlier Gilkey Hall Jr. had led his mates in prayer as they passed on the way overseas; Hall and his brother Daniel Kerp Hall both were killed. (Information from Marie Smith; stories in *Real Heroes*.)

S/Sgt. Charlie M. Whitaker, left, Headquarters Company/125th Engineers/14th Armored Division, served in the Rhineland and Central Europe as a construction foreman. He was one of five Whitaker brothers who served in the World War II. He earned the American Theater, the EAME Campaign Medal, the Good Conduct Medal, and the World War II Victory Medal. Pvt. Morris Claude Whitaker, right, 599th Field Artillery Battalion/45th Division, served in Germany after the occupation; he received the Occupation Medal. (Courtesy of Ruth Whitaker.)

S/Sgt. Vannoy Bright, right, Battery B/8th Field Artillery Observation Battalion, was a brother of S/Sgt. Leroy Bright, a paratrooper killed in the Battle of the Bulge; information on S/Sgt. Leroy Bright is in *Real Heroes*. Spindale mayor Jack Metcalf told the *Courier* that he remembered Vannoy as "a soldier in every respect" and that the Town of Spindale was proud of Vannoy's efforts; Mayor Metcalf ordered the flags flown at half-mast in honor of Vannoy and other servicemen on June 3, 1983. (Photo courtesy of Mavis Bridges; information courtesy of the *Daily Courier* and Jim Brown.)

Capt. Charles Burrington Long, a chaplain with the 7th Army, participated in nine battles in Italy, France, and Germany, including the Battle of the Bulge. Chaplain Long left behind two sons and a wife. Captain Long was Methodist. He remained in Germany until 1947 and was able to bring his family with him. (Courtesy of Mr. and Mrs. George Long.)

T/5 Walter H. Edwards, 86th Quartermaster Company, expedited supplies to the front line. His awards include the Asiatic-Pacific Campaign Medal, the American Theater, the EAME Campaign Medal with one Bronze Service Star, the Good Conduct Medal, and the World War II Victory Medal. (Courtesy of Walter H. Edwards.)

While visiting Ulm, Pvt. Arthur L. Roach, left, Company E/141st Infantry Regiment/36th Division, poses with fellow soldier Roger. Private Roach wrote on the photo that after the bombing, most of the town looked like this house. "America should be happy it is not like this." Private Roach was the nephew of T/5. General Morgan Horton (page 37). (Courtesy of Eva Cole Horton Humphries.)

Sgt. Wayne Yelton, Company M/310th Infantry Regiment/78th Division, served in the heavy weapons company of his regiment. He participated in three battles and earned the Purple Heart, the Bronze Star Medal with cluster, the CIB, the American Theater Campaign Medal, the EAME Campaign Medal with three Bronze Service Stars, the Good Conduct Medal, and the World War II Victory Medal. His unit received the Presidential Unit Citation. (Courtesy of Wayne Yelton.)

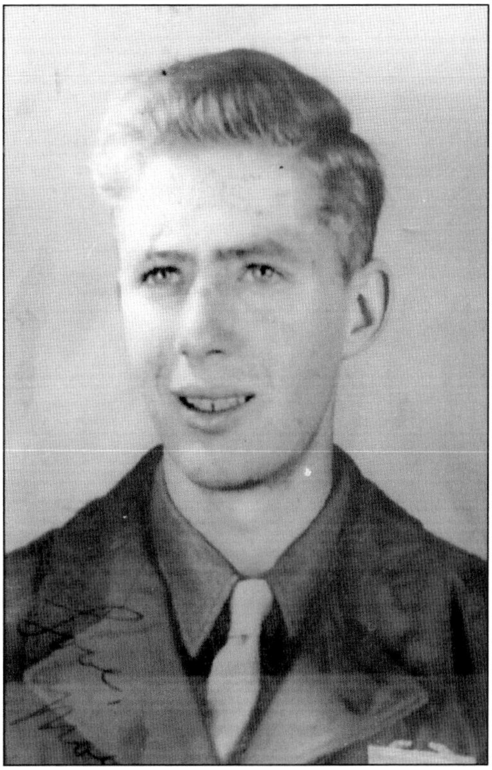

T/5 Norris Eugene Wells, Company C/808th Tank Destroyer Battalion, served in Northern France, the Ardennes, and Central Europe. He drove an M18 Tank Destroyer. Technician Wells suffered wounds in Luxembourg and received care in England. His most vivid memory was liberating a German concentration camp and witnessing the inhumanity. (Courtesy of Margaret Wells Brooks.)

T/5 Dean Bobo Scruggs, Company C/680th Quartermaster Company/107th General Hospital/7th Army, was a laundry machine operator who sanitized linens for the hospital. Following the advance of the forces, his unit ended in Garmisch-Partenkirchen, Germany. He earned the EAME Campaign Medal, the Good Conduct Medal, and the World War II Victory Medal. Scruggs is third from the left above. (Courtesy of Dean B. Scruggs.)

Pfc. Joe Reid Pinson, 119th Military Police Company (Aviation), served in Central Europe. He received the Bronze Star Medal, the EAME Campaign Medal with one Bronze Service Star, the Good Conduct Medal, and the World War II Victory Medal. (Courtesy of Valoree Harrill.)

Pfc. Thomas Earl Baldwin, 656th Tank Destroyer Battalion (SP) 9th Armored Division, helped capture the Ludendorf Bridge at Remagen, Germany, in March 1945. More information on Thomas Earl Baldwin is available in *Rutherford County in World War II: Volume I*, page 96. (Courtesy of Thomas Earl Baldwin.

Pvt. Hubert G. "Buddy" Wilkie, Company E/393rd Infantry Regiment/99th Division, crossed the Rhine on the Ludendorf Bridge on March 11, 1945, at Remagen, Germany. Under fire from enemy artillery and aircraft, the unit suffered losses during the crossing. Private Wilkie earned the CIB, the Bronze Star, the EAME Campaign Medal with two Bronze Service Stars, the Good Conduct Medal, the World War II Victory Medal, and the Army of Occupation Medal. He mustered out in 1979 as a captain. (Courtesy of H.G. Buddy Wilkie.)

(*above, left*) S/Sgt. Ward Randolph was killed in Germany on April 15, 1945. His information is included in *Real Heroes*. His marker reads, "He gave his life for his country in Germany. He is not dead; he is just asleep." (Courtesy of Douglas H. Hayes.) (*above, right*) Pfc. James B. Norville, right, served in the Army in Germany. He received his discharge in 1945. (Courtesy of Sylvia L. Hedin.)

Cpl. Thomas Paul Phillips, Battery A 790th Field Artillery Battalion, served in Central Europe and in Germany in the postwar occupation. He told his son of visiting a concentration camp and seeing the fingernail marks that the prisoners had made while on the wall trying to escape. Corporal Phillips guarded work details of German POWs. When Phillips was leaving Germany, he was supposed to drive a jeep; another soldier begged Phillips for the detail. The other soldier and passengers died when the vehicle exploded a mine. (Courtesy of Gary Phillips.)

T/Sgt. Arthur M. Atchley, Headquarters Company/5th Armored Division, was a high-speed radio operator. He participated in Normandy, Northern France, the Ardennes, the Rhineland, and Central Europe. He received the American Defense Service Medal, the EAME Campaign Medal with three Bronze Service Stars, and the Good Conduct Medal; his unit received the Distinguished Unit Citation. He poses wearing the decorations of a captured German major general. (Courtesy of Doug Atchley Jr.)

(*left*) Cpl. Robert Lewis Frazier, left, 1st Platoon/Company A/26th Infantry Division, crossed the Rhine on a pontoon bridge. "From there we didn't stop. With General Patton leading the way, through big towns and small villages, we captured all . . . When we did stop we were in Linz, Austria." Corporal Frazier, armed with a Browning automatic rifle, stands among the dragon teeth and the Siegfried line. (Courtesy of Robert L. Frazier.) (*right*) Pfc. Baxter E. White, Company B 329th Infantry Regiment 83rd Division, earned his CIB in the Ardennes, the Rhineland, and Central Europe. He received the EAME Campaign Medal with three Bronze Service Stars, the Good Conduct Medal, and the World War II Victory Medal. (Courtesy of Janice White.)

Grady Lee Henson, left, 11th Infantry Regiment/5th Division, entered service in 1940. Sergeant Henson earned the CIB and Bronze Star while participating in the Rhineland and Central Europe. He retired as a Sergeant First Class after 25 years. His brother is Pfc. Oscar Herman Henson, right, who served as a supply clerk in the 7223rd Supply Squadron. During his postwar occupation duties, he was able to get along very well with the German people. He won the CIB, the EAME Campaign Medal, and the Good Conduct Medal. He served from 1944 until 1968. (Courtesy of Oscar H. Henson.)

T/4 Bryan L. Basden, 2nd Platoon/Company M/319th Infantry Regiment/80th Division, served in the Ardennes, the Rhineland, and Central Europe. In Germany, Basden pushed as far east as Chemitz, south of Berlin. They met the Red Army, turned south, and went through Nuremberg before ending the war in Steyr, Austria. He earned the Purple Heart, three CIBs, the EAME with three Bronze Service Stars, the Good Conduct Medal, and the World War II Victory Medal. His unit captured the above bridge intact near Erfurt, Germany. Also serving in Germany were Gordon Carver, a supply sergeant at Bremerhaven, Germany, and his brother Keith Carver, who served in the Military Police in Germany; they are two of five Carver brothers who served in World War II. (Courtesy of B.L. Basden.)

Capt. Max G. Edwards, Company M/3rd Battalion/405th Infantry Regiment/102nd Division, vividly remembers as his unit advanced across the north German plain near Gardeleben, they came upon 1,032 men who had been burned by the Germans while the Germans were retreating. He recalls a miracle when his friend Henry ran "through bullets as thick as a dog's hair" to aid a friend. "My Lord walked on water, but Henry ran through the bullets." (Courtesy of Max G. Edwards.)

Capt. Max G. Edwards was one of the officers designated to meet the Red Army at the Elbe River; he reported to Allied Command Headquarters on conditions in the Russian zone of occupation. Captain Edwards was the recipient of a Bronze Star. (Courtesy of Max G. Edwards.)

(*above, left*) The Germans captured Cpl. Jack Pickford Huskey, Troop A/87th Cavalry Reconnaissance/7th Armored Division, on the October 27, 1944 in Northern France, near the German border. He remained a POW until the Russians liberated him on April 25, 1945. He earned the American Service Medal, the EAME Campaign Medal with two Bronze Service Stars, the World War II Victory Medal, and the Good Conduct Medal. (Courtesy of Jacqueline H. Outten.) (*above, right*) Cpl. Robert L. Whisnant, right, Headquarters Company/10th Armored Infantry, was captured 30 days before the end of the war; his confinement was at Stalag VIIA. His awards include the CIB, the EAME Campaign Medal with three Bronze Service Stars, and the Good Conduct Medal. (Information courtesy of Bobby D. Whisnant.)

Pfc. Floyd Leonard Radford, Company L/26th Infantry Regiment 1st Division, originally joined the 94th Division. He served in the Rhineland and Central Europe. At the end of the war, because of his excellent service, he received a transfer assignment to the 1st Division, where he received appointment as a guard at the International Military Tribunal at Nuremberg. Private Radford was in the courtroom as a guard during the Nuremberg War Crimes Trials. His most vivid recollections were that "Herman Goring had large fat fingers, and Rudolf Hess had bright blue eyes." Private Radford's brother Howard was a captain in the USAAF and later a doctor in the Cliffside area; his brother Lt. James Earl Radford was a bombardier. (Courtesy of Floyd L. Radford.)

Ben Teilman's parents gave him to a Protestant family in August 1940 for protection after the Nazi occupation. His mother died in Bergen-Belsen; his father died in Auschwitz-Birkenau. Ben remembers the liberation of Groningen by Canadian soldiers and looking up and seeing a "big red soldier." The soldier gave him a piece of chocolate that he thought was mud, an egg, and a piece of white bread. Ben was in the Guard of Honor of the Queen of Holland and is an honorary member of the Henrietta American Legion Post 423. Ben says, "Inhale your freedom. Embrace those who gave it to you." (Courtesy of Ben and Suzette Tielman.

George Pintoff, right, 4th Marine Division, was one of those who crossed the black volcanic sands of Iwo Jima. He recalls with intense grief "the loss of most of his unit." Pintoff retired from the Marines as a major. He participated in the Korean War, saw action at Pork Chop Hill with the 1st Marine Division, and received wounds twice during his military career. He earned the Navy Cross. (Courtesy of Lyles Mason, who appears on the left.)

(*above, left*) The final major battle of the Pacific was the conquest of Okinawa. Cpl. James Clarence Coffey served in the Marines from June 29, 1943, through December 4, 1945. After the war he entered the Marine Corps Reserve until June 21, 1947. He participated in Okinawa. (Courtesy of Hannah C. Baynard.) (*above, right*) Motor Machinist's Mate 1/C Robert Q. Womick served aboard LSM 120; he participated in Okinawa. He earned the American Campaign Service Medal, the EAME Campaign Medal, the Asiatic-Pacific Campaign Medal, the Occupation of Japan Medal, the World War II Victory Medal, and the Good Conduct Medal. (Courtesy of Robert Q. Womick.)

S/Sgt. Billy B. Baber, Company B 733rd Amphibious Tractor Battalion, participated in Leyte Gulf, Luzon, Ie Shima, Keise, and Okinawa. Sergeant Baber's battalion transferred troops from the attack transports to the beaches and lent support fire for the invading forces. Following the surrender, Sergeant Baber served six months in Japan with the occupation. He earned the Asiatic-Pacific Campaign Medal, the Philippine Liberation Medal, and the Good Conduct Medal. (Courtesy of Billy B. Baber.)

Cpl. A.C. Burgess, Company H/382nd Infantry Regiment/96th Division, was a forward observer for a 81mm mortar and survived three banzai charges. He remembers how during Okinawa he would help comfort the mortally wounded by praying with them as they died. He earned the CIB, the Asiatic-Pacific Campaign Medal, two Bronze Arrowheads, the Philippine Liberation Medal, the World War II Victory Medal, and the Good Conduct Medal. (Courtesy of A.C. Burgess.)

Cpl. Charles Jackson Condrey, 1st Battalion/4th Regiment/6th Marine Division, recalls many horrendous moments of combat. He remembers fellow Marine Guy Morehead's severe wound. His unit received the Presidential Unit Citation for its heroism. (Courtesy of Charles Jackson Condrey.)

(*above, left*) Lee Roy Logan served aboard the USS *Aurelia*, an attack transport ship that helped deliver the invasion forces to the beaches. Logan participated in Okinawa on Easter Sunday, April 1, 1945, and the occupation of Japan. For his services he received the Asiatic-Pacific Campaign Medal and the World War II Victory Medal. (Courtesy of Lee Roy Logan.) (*above, far right*) Sgt. Frank Brown, 459th Aviation Squadron, served as winch operator in the Ryukyu Islands. He earned the Asiatic-Pacific Service Medal with one Bronze Service Star, the World War II Victory Medal, the Occupation of Okinawa Medal, and the Good Conduct Medal. (Courtesy of Frank Brown.)

(*above, left*) Pfc. Virgil L. Lowery, 86th Field Hospital, was reluctant to talk of his Okinawa experiences. His relatives believe that he had the necessary but unpleasant duty of stitching body bags before burials. He received the American Theater Campaign Medal, the Asiatic-Pacific Campaign Medal with one Bronze Service Star, and the World War II Victory Medal. (Courtesy of Johnny Lowery.) (*above, far right*) Cpl. Ishel E. Gosey, Headquarters Battery/52nd Field Artillery Battalion, served as a heavy truck driver. Corporal Gosey received the Asiatic-Pacific Campaign Medal, the Philippine Liberation Medal, the World War II Victory Medal, the Occupation of Japan Ribbon, and the Good Conduct Medal. (Courtesy of Debbie Gosey.)

Nine

JAPAN SURRENDERS (1945); THE HOME FRONT (1941–1945)

Doing Our Part

With the successful occupation of Okinawa, plans were underway for the invasion of Japan. This proposed invasion that would have brought about hundreds of thousands of casualties on both sides became unnecessary because of the use of the atomic bomb. After the destruction of Hiroshima and Nagasaki, the Japanese surrendered on August 15, 1945. The Allies and Japanese representatives signed the formal surrender on board the USS Missouri *on September 2, 1945.*

The above photograph, courtesy of Charles Jack Condrey, shows Adm. Chester W. Nimitz, Commander-in-Chief of the Pacific Fleet, signing the acceptance of surrender. Gen. Douglas MacArthur, hands behind back, witnesses the signature.

First Lt. Grover H. Bradley, third from left in back, 485th Squadron/315th Bomb Wing/501st Bomb Group/20th Air Force, in his B-29 *Punch and Jody* flew one of the very last combat missions of World War II. Leaving from Guam on August 14, 1945, the plane attacked an oil refinery on the northern part of Honshu Island. By the time the crew had returned to their base on August 15, 1945, the Japanese had surrendered. Bradley's unit had the honor of circling at 3,000 feet the USS *Missouri* during the surrender ceremonies. His awards include the Air Medal with three stars; his unit received two Presidential Unit Citations. (Courtesy of Grover H. Bradley.)

S1/C Bill E. Beatty was aboard the USS *Ault* in Tokyo Bay during the surrender ceremonies. Beatty saw the event as a great day for his crew and the world. Beatty earned the American Area Campaign Medal, the Asiatic-Pacific Campaign Medal with four Bronze Service Stars, the Philippine Liberation Medal with one Bronze Service Star, and the World War II Victory Medal. (Courtesy of Bill E. Beatty.)

(*above, left*) Pfc. Wilbert W. Bright, Company E/119th Infantry Regiment, served as a cook. He participated in the Philippines and the occupation of Japan and for his services earned the Asiatic-Pacific Campaign Medal, the World War II Victory Medal, the Occupation of Japan Medal, and the Good Conduct Medal. (Courtesy of Wilbert Bright.) (*above, right*) Pfc. James A. Leach, Company K/391st Infantry Regiment/98th Division, told his son of the rough Pacific crossing when he served as a replacement soldier. He served in the Japanese occupation forces. Leach earned the American Theater Service Medal, the Asiatic-Pacific Campaign Medal, the World War II Victory Medal, and the Good Conduct Medal. (Courtesy of Steve Leach.)

(*above, left*) Pfc. T.F. Kelly, left, 22nd Regiment/6th Marines, received orders for Tsingtao, China, to accept the surrender of Japanese forces. He remained in China for one year and returned to San Diego in August 1946. (Courtesy of T.F. Kelly and family.) (*above, right*) Cpl. Roy L. McKain, Company A/1st Battalion/5th Regiment/1st Marine Division, protected an ammunition supply depot at Hsin Ho, China. The Marines suffered five killed in the action of April 15, 1947, and received 16 Purple Hearts after the attack of Chinese Communists. He received, among others, the Good Conduct Medal and the National China Medal. (Courtesy of Roy McKain.)

(*above, left*) T/5 Foy Lee Crow served in the Merchant Marines as a fireman, a water tender, and an oiler. He also served in the Army Medical Corps in Tokyo. (Courtesy of Foy Lee Crow.) (*above, right*) Petty Officer 3/C William O. Wells served aboard the USS *Frank Knox*. The *Knox* was a radar picket destroyer. His fondest memory was of meeting Paul Wells, going through basic training with him, serving with him on three separate ships, being discharged at the same time, and having remained friends for 50 years. He earned the Occupation of Japan Medal, the U.S. Korean Service, the United Nations Korean Service, and the Good Conduct Medal. (Courtesy of William O. Wells.)

(*above, left*) Charles A. Baynard retired as a master sergeant after service in the 1st Air Force and the 14th Air Force. He served from February 1946 until August 1966 and received commendation for his service. (Courtesy of Charles A. Baynard.) (*above, right*) Sgt. George Earl Jolley served in Fairbanks, Alaska, in the Army Air Forces as an airplane maintenance technician. For his services he earned the American Theater Service Medal, the Asiatic-Pacific Campaign Medal, the World War II Victory Medal, and the Good Conduct Medal. He also received commendation for services under severe conditions particular to Alaska and Canada. (Courtesy of Sarah H. Jolley.)

T/4 Joe Dobbins, 254th Military Police Company, served in Whitehorse, Yukon Territory, and on the Alcan Highway for 2 and one-half years. He earned the World War II Victory Medal and the Good Conduct Medal. He is the brother-in-law of Ralph Bridges, who appears on page 59. (Courtesy of Joe Dobbins.)

Pfc. John T. Medford served in the 555th Military Police E.G. Company. The duty of his unit was to guard German and Italian POWs at Camp Winegarten, Farmington, Missouri. He and his fellow soldiers patrolled the perimeters on motorcycles. He earned the American Theater Campaign Medal, the Asiatic-Pacific Campaign Medal, the World War II Victory Medal, and the Good Conduct Medal. Serving in the same unit was Joe Bridges who appears later in this chapter. (Courtesy of John T. Medford.)

(*above, left*) Sgt. A. Arnold Atchley, brother of James Horace and Hubert Atchley, served in Mississippi and Texas as a drill sergeant. (Courtesy of Elizabeth A. Harrison.) (*above, right*) Pvt. Collon James Phillips also served stateside in the 493rd Heavy Ordnance Maintenance Company. Many health problems plagued Phillips's during his time in service. (Courtesy of Collon James Phillips.)

(*above, left*) Pfc. James Madison Moss, 37th Base Headquarters Base Squadron, served as Military Police at the New Orleans Army Air Forces Base. His discharge paper makes note of Madison's excellent character. (Courtesy of Nell J. Moss.) (*above, right*) Pvt. Ray Daniel Lowery, 171st Evacuation Hospital, was a truck driver who transported the wounded to the hospital at Fort Bragg. He received the World War II Victory Medal. (Courtesy of Billy Seay.)

Cpl. Mike J. Williams, left, Cannon Company/108th Infantry Regiment, served in the Panama Canal Zone, the Hawaiian Islands, and Guadalcanal. He earned the American Theater Campaign Medal, the Asiatic-Pacific Campaign Medal, and the Good Conduct Medal. S/1C. Mary Lee Humphries, right, served in transportation at Navy Air Station, Norfolk, Virginia, and at Edenton, North Carolina. She earned the American Campaign Medal and the World War II Victory Medal. Later the two married. (Courtesy of Mary Lee Humphries Williams.)

(*above, left*) Pfc. Theodore L. Walker, Company A/62nd Infantry Training Battalion, helped train soldiers at Fort Sill, Oklahoma, for duties overseas. He earned the Good Conduct Medal. (Courtesy of Evelyn W. Moore.) (*above, right*) T/5 Roy V. Hyder, 762nd AAA SLT Battery, served as a control station operator. For his services Hyder received the American Theater Campaign Medal, the Asiatic-Pacific Campaign Medal, the World War II Victory Medal, and the Good Conduct Medal. His son R. Vaughan Hyder (994 Piedmont Road, Rutherfordton, NC 28139-7367; phone 828-287-5441) pleads for any information on his dad. (Courtesy of Vaughan Hyder.)

(*above, left*) S/Sgt. Albert Reid Bridges, left, 3501st Army Air Force Base Unit, was a pharmacy technician. He earned American Defense Service Medal, the American Theater Service Medal, the World War II Victory Medal, and the Good Conduct Medal. After the war, Bridges owned the Smith's Drug Store in Rutherfordton, North Carolina, for 33 years. (*above, right*) Lt. Horace V. Doggett was a brother-in-law of Albert Reid Bridges, Hubert Bridges, and Don Burrell Bridges. He was an airplane pilot at Craig Field, Selma, Alabama. (Both photos courtesy of Mavis Bridges.)

(*above, left*) Pvt. Ralph Clyde Cannon served in the Army at Camp Polk, Louisiana. He was drafted at the age of 38. (*above, right*) His younger brother Clarence Louis "Jud" Cannon, 5th Squadron/9th Bomb Group/20th Air Force, served on Tinian Island. He received the Asiatic-Pacific Campaign Medal with three Bronze Service Stars. His unit earned two Presidential Unit Citations. (Both photos courtesy of Helen Byers.)

S1/C Max Morris Robbins was a Special Artificer (Special Devices) in the Navy. Robbins helped train aviators for the Navy at Naval Air Station, San Diego. He used a link trainer as a simulator for the pilots-to-be. Robbins was the son of Mr. and Mrs. L.B. Robbins. (Courtesy of Mrs. Wanda Robbins.)

Clark Robbins, brother of S1/C Max Morris Robbins, was a storekeeper assigned to a supply depot in Pennsylvania. Clark Robbins began Navy service in September of 1940. He had a Reserve Pilot Training Commission. He transferred to inactive status for 10–15 years. Robbins was the son of Mr. and Mrs. L.B. Robbins. (Courtesy of Mrs. Wanda Robbins.)

S1/C Thomas Gene Brooks served aboard the USS *Franklin D. Roosevelt*. Seaman Brooks's duty was to move the aircraft between the flight deck and the hangar deck. He had an appendectomy while aboard the *Franklin D. Roosevelt*. (Courtesy of Gene Brooks.)

Selma Walker, later the wife of T.G. Brooks, worked with Southern Bell Telephone Company as an operator during the war and thereafter. She recalled how the operators made every effort to connect the service personnel with their families when they called. Pictured with Selma is her twin brother Elmer Walker, who served in the Navy at Naval Air Station, Corpus Christi, Texas. (Courtesy of Selma Walker Brooks.)

(*above, left*) Selma and Elmer's other brother, CPO Robert S. Walker, served for 42 years in the Navy. He served at a number of naval air stations as a flight engineer. (Courtesy of Selma Walker Brooks.) (*above, right*) S1c Joe Webb served aboard the U.S.S. *Cushing* during the last months of the war in the Southwest Pacific. (Courtesy of Nell Webb and Gertrude Silver.)

(*above left*) S1c Dan E. King arrived in Hawaii on August 15, 1945, the day the Japanese surrendered. He worked in the flight scheduling office at the John Rogers Naval Air Station, Honolulu, Hawaii. King's unit helped to arrange transportation to the United States via aircraft for seriously wounded service personnel. (Courtesy of Dan E. King.) (*above, right*) Lt. (jg) Charles Vance Abernathy served as a dentist to military personnel. He tended to those in the U.S. Army, U.S. Navy, and U.S. Marine Corps. (Courtesy of Charles V. Abernathy.)

(*above, left*) Sgt. Max D. Hicks served in the 28th Cavalry Reconnaissance Squadron in Italy, France, and Germany. During the last months of the war this unit was attached to Lt. Gen. George S. Patton's 3rd Army. For his service he received the EAME Campaign Medal and the Good Conduct Medal. (*above, right*) His brother Charles Hicks served in the Army during World War II. Their sister Reba Hicks married Max Ferree, who served in the Navy. (Courtesy of Hicks family.)

(*above, left*) S/Sgt. Hydrick Lane, 601st Tactical Squadron, repaired radar equipment on the various types of planes. The first radar station—"Bookworm"—in postwar Germany was his station. He remained in service through the Berlin Airlift. Sergeant Lane married Lotte Suhr and brought her home with him. (Courtesy of Hydrick Lane.) (*above, right*) Maj. Solon D. Smart served with the Army Service Forces, Office of the Quartermaster General. Major Smart was a clothing and equipment distribution officer. For his services Major Smart earned the American Theater Service Medal, the American Defense Service Medal, and the World War II Victory Medal. A major road in Rutherford County bears his name in recognition of his service to the county. (Courtesy of Douglas Hayes.)

(*above, left photo on right*) Pharmacist's Mate 3/C Virginia E. Burgess Schwartz served in the Hospital Corps of the WAVES from 1945 through 1947. She served at the Naval Hospital in Norfolk, Virginia, and the Naval Hospital in New York. (Courtesy of Virginia E. Burgess Schwartz.) (*above, right*) Willie "Sunshine" Toms Tedder was in the Cadet Nurse Corps at the Baptist Hospital in Winston-Salem, North Carolina. Sunshine, right, remembers how her boyfriend John Tedder came to see her before he went home to see his parents. The end of the war came before Sunshine's nursing program/State Boards were complete. (Courtesy of Sunshine Toms Tedder.)

(*above, left*) Sunshine's father-in-law and John Tedder's father was Edward S. Tedder, engineer for the Seaboard Airline Railway. Tedder often carried troops from Rutherfordton, North Carolina, to Hamlet, North Carolina. (*above, right*) Serving with him as fireman was Edward Rollins Price, who later became engineer also. Ed Price was the brother of Arthur F. Price, who was killed on December 28, 1944. More information on Corporal Price is available on page 153 in *Real Heroes*. Ed was also the brother of Falls W. Price and Roy D. Price who are in *Rutherford County in World War II: Volume I*, pages 74, 76, and 81; Arthur Price is on page 116 in the same volume. (Courtesy of John Tedder and Ed Price.)

Pictured are, from left to right, Joe Bridges; Eva Bridges, later wife of John G. Pruette; John G. Pruett, who is on page 52 of this volume; and Bill Bridges. Joe Bridges served with John Medford in the 555th Military Police E.G. Company. He guarded German and Italian POWs at Camp Winegarten, Farmington, Missouri. He and his fellow soldiers patrolled the perimeters on motorcycles. Bill Bridges was in the USAAF. His B-24 crashed as a result of enemy fire, and he suffered internment in Switzerland until the end of the war. (Courtesy of Eva B. Pruette.)

Cpl. James W. Logan, at console, served with Southeast Training Command U.S. Army Air Corps. Corporal Logan trained aerial gunners on individually mounted and turret mounted .50-caliber machine guns. In Fort Myers, Florida, he used a five-camera setup that would simulate a 3-D image of an attacking aircraft. (Courtesy of James W. Logan.)